This book belongs to

....

Date

....

An All-in-One Study
on Salvation and New Life

romans

An All-in-One Study on Salvation and New Life

romans

THE BIBLE STUDY COLLECTIVE

BARBOUR PUBLISHING

Editorial assistance by Tracy M. Sumner and Carey Scott.

ISBN 979-8-89151-169-9

Published by Barbour Publishing, Inc., 1810 Barbour Drive, Uhrichsville, Ohio 44683, www.barbourbooks.com

Our mission is to inspire the world with the life-changing message of the Bible.

ecpa Member of the Evangelical Christian Publishers Association

Printed in China.

Contents

THE BIBLE STUDY COLLECTIVE

Welcome to *Romans: An All-in-One Study on Salvation and New Life,* a collection of thirty select passages from the book of Romans as well as guidance and encouragement for digging into them yourself. The Epistle to the Romans is the first of the apostle Paul's thirteen letters to appear in the New Testament canon. It describes the gospel of Jesus Christ, starting with sinful humanity's need for a savior to reconcile them to God. This amazing letter presents the gospel as God's act of salvation for both Jews and Gentiles who believe in Christ's death and resurrection.

Each study in this guide includes an introduction of the particular passage of Romans on the first page, followed by the full text of the passage on the next. The third through the fifth pages of each study highlight the three steps of what is called the "inductive method" of Bible study: observation, interpretation, and application. Here's how it works:

- *Observation* answers the question "What does it say?" In other words, what is the actual content in the text?
- *Interpretation* answers the question "What does it mean?" In this step, you'll consider the author's original intent and meaning.
- Finally, *application* answers the questions "What does it mean to you—and how can you apply it to your life?"

Each study in this guide ends with a select verse (or verses) from the Romans passage you've just studied, as well as related scriptures for memorization and meditation.

Our prayer is that *Romans: An All-in-One Study on Salvation and New Life* will help you to better understand God's Word, and to apply its timeless truth to your own life of faith in the Lord Jesus Christ.

Barbour Publishing

Study 1

ROMANS 1:1–17

The book of Romans opens with two introductions: the apostle Paul introducing himself and his gospel, both to the Roman Christians. Paul lets the church know that God Himself had called him and set him aside to preach the gospel of Jesus Christ, the Messiah promised to humankind centuries before His arrival.

Paul declared that, although he was a Jew, he was "not ashamed" of the gospel of Christ and introduced the Romans to the radical, life-changing, eternity-altering theme of this letter: being made right with God (justification) on the basis of faith in Jesus (verses 16–17).

Romans 1:1–17 Study Outline

(VERSE 1)	Paul introduces himself to the Roman Christians
(VERSES 2–6)	Paul introduces his gospel to the Romans
(VERSES 7–15)	Paul's desire to visit the Christians in Rome
(VERSES 16–17)	The theme of Paul's letter to the Romans

Paul's Life Calling

1Paul, a servant of Jesus Christ, called to be an apostle, sep-
arated to the gospel of God, 2which He had promised before
by His prophets in the holy scriptures, 3concerning His Son,
Jesus Christ our Lord, who was born of a descendant of David
according to the flesh, 4and declared to be the Son of God with
power, according to the Spirit of holiness, by the resurrection
from the dead. 5By Him we have received grace and apostleship
for obedience to the faith among all nations for His name,
6among whom you are also the called of Jesus Christ. 7To all
who are in Rome, beloved of God, called to be saints: grace and
peace to you from God our Father and the Lord Jesus Christ.

8First, I thank my God through Jesus Christ for you all,
that your faith is spoken of throughout the whole world. 9For
God, whom I serve with my spirit in the gospel of His Son, is
my witness that without ceasing I always make mention of
you in my prayers, 10making request, if by any means, now,
finally, I might have a prosperous journey by the will of God
to come to you.

11For I long to see you, that I may impart some spiritual
gift to you, to the end you may be established—12that is, that
I may be comforted together with you by the mutual faith of
both you and me. 13Now I do not want to have you ignorant,
brothers, that oftentimes I purposed to come to you (but was
hindered until now), that I might have some fruit among you
also, even as among other Gentiles.

14I am a debtor both to the Greeks and to the barbarians,
both to the wise and to the unwise. 15So, as much as is in me,
I am ready to preach the gospel to you also who are at Rome.

16For I am not ashamed of the gospel of Christ, for it is the
power of God for salvation to everyone who believes, to the
Jew first and also to the Greek. 17For in it the righteousness of
God is revealed from faith to faith, as it is written, "The just
shall live by faith."

Observe

How does Paul describe himself in the opening verse of Romans 1?

What was Paul's heart attitude toward the gospel of Christ?

Who was the gospel message for, according to verse 16?

Interpret

What did Paul mean when he referred to himself as "separated to the gospel of God"?

Which important doctrines does Paul communicate in verses 2–4? What do they mean?

What does it mean that Jesus was "declared to be the Son of God" by the resurrection?

Apply

How does your attitude toward fellow believers today compare or contrast with Paul's attitude toward the Roman Christians?

Have you ever felt afraid or ashamed to share the gospel with others? Why?

How important do you think it is to share the gospel with others? What might give you the confidence to do so with boldness?

Romans 1:1–17 Scriptures for Memorization/Meditation

For I am not ashamed of the gospel of Christ,
for it is the power of God for salvation to everyone
who believes, to the Jew first and also to the Greek.
VERSE 16

"The just shall live by faith."
VERSE 17

Verses for Further Memorization/Meditation

- "Let your light so shine before men, that they may see your good works and glorify your Father who is in heaven" (Matthew 5:16).
- "And now, Lord, behold their threats and grant to Your servants that they may speak Your word with all boldness" (Acts 4:29).
- Therefore be followers of God as dear children, and walk in love, as Christ has also loved us and has given Himself for us, an offering and a sacrifice to God for a sweet-smelling savor (Ephesians 5:1–2).

Study 2

ROMANS 1:18–28

The book of Romans is filled with good news for humankind: that God made a way for our salvation apart from anything we could do to earn or deserve it. But before Paul explains and describes God's incredible act of grace and mercy, he first gives us the bad news: every one of us is guilty before God and well deserving of His wrath.

We should—without exception—experience His full anger and eternal punishment for our unrighteousness before Him, and Romans 1:18–28 describes in detail why that is an inescapable, terrible truth for everyone born into this world.

That is surely horrible news. But there is hope for all of us, hope that Paul will describe as this letter continues.

Romans 1:18–28 Study Outline

(VERSE 18)	Why we need to be justified: our guilt before God
(VERSES 19–23)	Demonstrations of human unrighteousness
(VERSES 24–25)	The tragic results of our guilt before God
(VERSES 26–28)	The descent into sin

A Guilty World

[18]For the wrath of God is revealed from heaven against all
ungodliness and unrighteousness of men, who hold the truth
in unrighteousness, [19]because what may be known of God is
evident in them, for God has shown it to them. [20]For from the
creation of the world the invisible things of Him are clearly
seen, being understood by the things that are made, even His
eternal power and Godhead, so that they are without excuse,
[21]because when they knew God, they did not glorify Him as
God, nor were thankful, but became vain in their imaginations,
and their foolish hearts were darkened. [22]Professing them-
selves to be wise, they became fools [23]and changed the glory
of the incorruptible God into an image made like corruptible
man and to birds and four-footed beasts and creeping things.

[24]Therefore God also gave them up to uncleanness through
the lusts of their own hearts, to dishonor their own bodies
between themselves, [25]who changed the truth of God into a
lie and worshipped and served the creature more than the
Creator, who is blessed forever. Amen.

[26]For this reason God gave them up to vile affections. For
even their women changed the natural use into what is against
nature, [27]and likewise the men also, leaving the natural use of
the woman, burned in their lust toward one another; men with
men working what is unseemly and receiving in themselves
the recompense that was fitting of their error.

[28]And even as they did not like to retain God in their
knowledge, God gave them over to a reprobate mind, to do
those things that are not proper.

ROMANS 1:18–28

Observe

For what does God show His anger, according to Romans 1:18–19?

....

....

....

....

....

Why would people not honor God, even though they could see He is real?

....

....

....

....

....

....

What phrase is repeated three times from verses 24 through 28?

....

....

....

....

....

....

Interpret

What does "what may be known of God is evident in them" mean?

What does "God also gave them up to uncleanness through the lusts of their own hearts" mean? Did God cause people to sin?

According to this passage, is there any legitimate excuse for not believing in God?

Apply

Where do you see the thoughts and behaviors described in this passage happening in the world today?

How should you respond to the wonders of God's creation?

How can you apply the truths in this passage to help you effectively share the gospel message with others?

Romans 1:18–28 Scripture for Memorization/Meditation

For from the creation of the world the invisible things of Him are clearly seen, being understood by the things that are made, even His eternal power and Godhead, so that they are without excuse.
VERSE 20

Verses for Further Memorization/Meditation

- And we have all received of His fullness, and grace for grace. For the law was given by Moses, but grace and truth came by Jesus Christ. No man has seen God at any time. The only begotten Son, who is in the bosom of the Father, He has declared Him (John 1:16–18).
- The heavens declare the glory of God, and the firmament shows His handiwork (Psalm 19:1).
- For God has appointed us not to wrath but to obtain salvation by our Lord Jesus Christ, who died for us, that, whether we wake or sleep, we should live together with Him (1 Thessalonians 5:9–10).

Study 3

ROMANS 2:1–16

Nearly everyone has some standard of morality. We know it's wrong to kill or otherwise harm another person. We know it's not right to steal, cheat, or lie. We mostly learn those moral standards from our families or from other important people in our lives.

But hypocrisy is a part of the fallen human condition, even for those of the finest moral training. We can scarcely hold to our low human standards of right and wrong, let alone to God's perfect standard of true righteousness.

We all violate the standards of behavior we set for ourselves—and especially for others. But more importantly, we all violate God's moral law, meaning we are without excuse. . .and fully worthy of God's righteous judgment.

Romans 2:1–16 Study Outline

(VERSES 1–3)	Flawed human morality
(VERSES 4–5)	God's judgment against the imperfectly moral
(VERSES 6–10)	The moral human's works fall short of God's perfect standard
(VERSES 11–13)	God's impartiality
(VERSES 14–16)	Possession of the law is of no advantage

Imperfect Human Standards of Morality

1Therefore you are inexcusable, O man, whoever you are who
judges, for in whatever you judge another you condemn your-
self. For you who judge do the same things. 2But we are sure
that the judgment of God is according to truth against those
who commit such things. 3And do you think this, O man, you
who judge those who do such things and do the same, that
you shall escape the judgment of God? 4Or do you despise the
riches of His goodness and patience and long-suffering, not
knowing that the goodness of God leads you to repentance?

5But according to your hardness and impenitent heart
you treasure up for yourself wrath toward the day of wrath
and revelation of the righteous judgment of God, 6who will
render to every man according to his deeds: 7to those who by
patient continuance in well-doing seek for glory and honor and
immortality—eternal life; 8but to those who are contentious and
do not obey the truth but obey unrighteousness—indignation
and wrath, 9tribulation and anguish on every soul of man who
does evil, of the Jew first and also of the Gentile; 10but glory,
honor, and peace to every man who works good, to the Jew first
and also to the Gentile. 11For there is no partiality with God.

12For as many as have sinned without law shall also perish
without law, and as many as have sinned in the law shall be
judged by the law. 13For the hearers of the law are not just
before God, but the doers of the law shall be justified. 14For
when the Gentiles, who do not have the law, by nature do the
things contained in the law, these, not having the law, are a
law to themselves, 15who show the work of the law written in
their hearts, their conscience also bearing witness, and their
thoughts meanwhile accusing or else excusing one another
16on the day when, according to my gospel, God shall judge
the secrets of men by Jesus Christ.

Observe

What does the word *judge* indicate in Romans 2? Why is it dangerous to pass judgment on others?

What, according to Romans 2:4, does God's goodness lead people to?

What will God one day judge, according to Romans 2:16?

Interpret

What words can describe the people referenced in this chapter—those who claim to be one thing while in reality being something else?

What does the phrase "For there is no partiality with God" say about His judgments?

Romans 2:13 says, "For the hearers of the law are not just before God, but the doers of the law shall be justified." What does that mean in light of the fact that no one keeps the law perfectly?

Apply

Why is it useful to know about God's judgment? How can that knowledge help you as you share the gospel?

What does it mean to you to be not just a *hearer* of God's word but also a *doer*? How can you make sure that you are a consistent doer?

How do you respond when you recognize God's goodness in your life?

Romans 2:1–16 Scripture for Memorization/Meditation

For there is no partiality with God. For as many as have sinned without law shall also perish without law, and as many as have sinned in the law shall be judged by the law. For the hearers of the law are not just before God, but the doers of the law shall be justified.
VERSES 11–13

Verses for Further Memorization/Meditation

- And all things are from God, who has reconciled us to Himself through Jesus Christ and has given to us the ministry of reconciliation—namely, that God was in Christ reconciling the world to Himself, not imputing their trespasses to them, and has committed to us the word of reconciliation (2 Corinthians 5:18–19).
- "He who believes in the Son has everlasting life, and he who does not believe the Son shall not see life, but the wrath of God remains on him" (John 3:36).
- The Lord is not slow concerning His promise, as some men count slowness, but is long-suffering toward us, not willing that any should perish but that all should come to repentance (2 Peter 3:9).

Study 4

ROMANS 2:17–29

In Romans 2:17–29, Paul addresses the "boast" of the Jewish people concerning their possession of the Law of Moses. The Jews of that time were extremely proud because God had given His law to their nation. They believed that their possession of the law confirmed their status as God's specially chosen people and ensured their salvation.

But although Paul acknowledged that the Jewish people should gratefully see the law as God's gift, he also held that mere possession of the law would not justify anyone.

To Paul, it came down to this: having the law means little if the people don't keep it perfectly—and no one, Jew or Gentile, kept the whole law flawlessly. They were all guilty before a holy and righteous God.

This passage drives home the fact that God will hold each of us accountable for both our heart's motives and our actions.

Romans 2:17–29 Study Outline

(VERSES 17–20)	The boast of the Jewish people
(VERSES 21–24)	The indictment against the hypocritical person
(VERSES 25–29)	The irrelevance of circumcision

Condemned by the Law

[17]Behold, you are called a Jew and rest in the law and make your boast in God, [18]and know His will and approve the things that are more excellent, being instructed out of the law, [19]and are confident that you yourself are a guide of the blind, a light to those who are in darkness, [20]an instructor of the foolish, a teacher of children, who have the form of knowledge and of the truth in the law.

[21]You therefore, who teach another, do you not teach yourself? You who preach that a man should not steal, do you steal? [22]You who say that a man should not commit adultery, do you commit adultery? You who abhor idols, do you commit sacrilege? [23]You who make your boast of the law, through breaking the law do you dishonor God? [24]For as it is written, "The name of God is blasphemed among the Gentiles through you."

[25]For circumcision truly profits if you keep the law, but if you are a breaker of the law, your circumcision is made uncircumcision. [26]Therefore if the uncircumcised man keeps the righteousness of the law, shall his uncircumcision not be counted for circumcision? [27]And shall uncircumcision that is by nature, if it fulfills the law, not judge you who, by the letter and circumcision, transgress the law?

[28]For he is not a Jew who is one outwardly, nor is circumcision that which is outward in the flesh. [29]But he is a Jew who is one inwardly—and circumcision is that of the heart, in the Spirit, and not in the letter—whose praise is not from men but from God.

Observe

On whom is Paul focused in this passage?

What is circumcision, and what is its significance in Old Testament law?

How was God's name blasphemed among the Gentiles because of the people of Israel?

Interpret

What does Paul mean when he refers to "the law"?

Under what circumstance was circumcision spiritually profitable for Jewish people?

What major problem does Paul point out in verses 21–23?

Apply

What "religious" activity in your own life parallels what Paul says about circumcision in this passage?

What kind of testimony does (and should) your life present to the world around you?

Based on these verses, what do you believe is most important to God?

Romans 2:17–29 Scriptures for Memorization/Meditation

You therefore, who teach another, do you not teach yourself? You who preach that a man should not steal, do you steal? You who say that a man should not commit adultery, do you commit adultery? You who abhor idols, do you commit sacrilege?
VERSES 21–22

For circumcision truly profits if you keep the law, but if you are a breaker of the law, your circumcision is made uncircumcision.
VERSE 25

Verses for Further Memorization/Meditation

- But be doers of the word and not hearers only, deceiving your own selves. For if any is a hearer of the word and not a doer, he is like a man looking at his natural face in a mirror. For he looks at himself and goes his way and immediately forgets what manner of man he was. But whoever looks into the perfect law of liberty and continues in it—not being a forgetful hearer but a doer of the work—this man shall be blessed in his deed (James 1:22–25).
- He who says "I know Him" and does not keep His commandments is a liar, and the truth is not in him. But whoever keeps His word, truly the love of God is perfected in him. By this we know that we are in Him: he who says he abides in Him ought himself also to walk even as He walked (1 John 2:4–6).
- For there are many unruly and vain talkers and deceivers, especially those of the circumcision, whose mouths must be stopped, who subvert whole houses teaching things that they ought not for filthy gain's sake (Titus 1:10–11).

Study 5

ROMANS 3:1–20

Romans 3:1–20 points out that, although the Hebrew people were privileged in God's entrusting them with the truth of His holy law, they would never be justified before Him on the basis of the law.

The law of God is a tremendous blessing, even to Gentiles today. But in and of itself, the law does not and cannot save us, any more than religious practices of any sort can save us. Rather, the law simply shows us that we can't attain righteousness on our own. It points us to the God who *can* save us through our faith.

Even though the Jewish people didn't faithfully follow God's perfect ways, He remained faithful to them as His covenant people. And though we today may be weak and unfaithful, God still demonstrates His love, His goodness, and His faithfulness to those who have come to Him on the basis of faith in Jesus Christ.

Romans 3:1–20 Study Outline

(VERSES 1–2)	The advantage of the Jewish people
(VERSES 3–4)	Jewish unbelief does not negate God's truth
(VERSES 5–8)	Human unrighteousness, and the righteousness of God
(VERSE 9)	The guilt of both Jew and Gentile
(VERSES 10–18)	The Old Testament assertions regarding the universal guilt of humankind
(VERSES 19–20)	The law cannot save us from the penalty of our sin

The Righteousness of God Demonstrated

1 Then what advantage does the Jew have? Or what is the profit
of circumcision?
2 Much in every way. Chiefly, because the oracles of God
were committed to them.
3 For what if some did not believe? Shall their unbelief
make the faithfulness of God without effect?
4 God forbid! Yes, let God be true but every man a liar. As
it is written, "That You might be justified in Your sayings and
might overcome when You are judged."
5 But if our unrighteousness demonstrates the righteous-
ness of God, what shall we say? Is God, who takes vengeance,
unrighteous? (I speak as a man.)
6 God forbid! For then how shall God judge the world?
7 For if through my lie the truth of God has more abounded
to His glory, why am I also still judged as a sinner?
8 And why not rather say (as we are slanderously reported
and as some affirm that we say), "Let us do evil that good may
come?" Their condemnation is just.
9 What then? Are we better than they? No, in no way. For
we have proved before that both Jews and Gentiles are all
under sin.
10 As it is written: "There is no one righteous, no, not one.
11 There is no one who understands; there is no one who
seeks after God.
12 They have all gone out of the way; they have together
become unprofitable. There is no one who does good. No,
not one."
13 "Their throat is an open sepulchre; with their tongues
they have used deceit." "The poison of asps is under their lips."
14 "Their mouth is full of cursing and bitterness."
15 "Their feet are swift to shed blood;
16 destruction and misery are in their ways,
17 and they have not known the way of peace."
18 "There is no fear of God before their eyes."

19 Now we know that whatever things the law says, it says
to those who are under the law, that every mouth may be
stopped and all the world may become guilty before God.
20 Therefore no flesh shall be justified in His sight by the
deeds of the law, for by the law is the knowledge of sin.

Observe

What does Paul say are the benefits of being a Jew?

What are both Jews and Gentiles under, according to Romans 3:9? What does that mean?

What is the purpose of the law, according to Romans 3:20?

Interpret

How is our unbelief related to God's faithfulness to His word and to His people?

What does it mean that the oracles of God were committed to the Jews (see verse 2)?

What does this passage say about our responsibility for our own unrighteousness?

Apply

How does this passage help you to better deal with your own sin and unbelief?

When sharing the gospel, how would you respond to someone who claims to be a good person without sin?

Why is it important to always speak the truth without lying?

Romans 3:1–20 Scriptures for Memorization/Meditation

As it is written: "There is no one righteous,
no, not one. There is no one who understands;
there is no one who seeks after God."
VERSES 10–11

Therefore no flesh shall be justified in His sight by the deeds of the law, for by the law is the knowledge of sin.
VERSE 20

Verses for Further Memorization/Meditation

- If we say that we have no sin, we deceive ourselves, and the truth is not in us (1 John 1:8).
- "We who are Jews by nature, and not sinners of the Gentiles, knowing that a man is justified not by the works of the law but by the faith of Jesus Christ, even we have believed in Jesus Christ, that we might be justified by the faith of Christ and not by the works of the law, for by the works of the law no flesh shall be justified" (Galatians 2:15–16).
- For as many as are of the works of the law are under the curse. For it is written: "Cursed is everyone who does not continue in all things that are written in the Book of the Law to do them" (Galatians 3:10).

Study 6

ROMANS 3:21–31

For the first two and a half chapters of the book of Romans, Paul makes the all-important point that human beings—Jews and Gentiles alike—are sinners who have no hope of earning salvation from the eternal consequences of their sin. Left to our own devices, we will all spiral into sin that continues to get worse and worse.

Now Paul shifts his focus toward the good news: God has lovingly and freely provided what only He can provide—righteousness and forgiveness for all our wrongdoing. Through Jesus' sacrificial death, we can be forgiven. And through our faith in Him, we can also be transformed into what we were not and could have never been.

ROMANS 3:21–31 STUDY OUTLINE

(VERSE 21)	The revelation of God's righteousness
(VERSE 22)	How God communicates His righteousness to humanity
(VERSES 23–24)	Humanity's universal need for God's gift of righteousness
(VERSES 25–26)	Jesus' sacrificial death satisfies God's righteous judgment
(VERSE 27)	There is nothing for humanity to boast about
(VERSES 28–31)	Justification is found apart from the deeds of the law

Our Source of Righteousness

21 But now the righteousness of God without the law is revealed,
being witnessed by the Law and the Prophets, 22 even the
righteousness of God that is by faith in Jesus Christ, to all
and on all those who believe. For there is no difference, 23 for
all have sinned and come short of the glory of God, 24 being
justified freely by His grace through the redemption that is
in Christ Jesus, 25 whom God has set forth to be a propitiation
in His blood, through faith, to declare His righteousness, for
the remission of sins that are past, through the patience of
God, 26 to declare, I say, at this time His righteousness, that He
might be just and the justifier of him who believes in Jesus.

27 Where is boasting then? It is excluded. By what law? Of
works? No, but by the law of faith. 28 Therefore we conclude
that a man is justified by faith without the deeds of the law. 29 Is
He the God of the Jews only? Is He not also of the Gentiles?
Yes, of the Gentiles also, 30 seeing it is one God who shall justify
the circumcised by faith and the uncircumcised through faith.
31 Do we then make void the law through faith? God forbid!
Yes, we establish the law.

Observe

By what is the righteousness of God imparted to us, according to Romans 3:22?

Who is truly without sin, according to Romans 3:23?

How are sinful people justified, according to Romans 3:24–26?

Interpret

What does the word *propitiation* mean, and why is it so important to the Christian faith?

What part do sinful people play in becoming righteous before God?

Since we all fall well short of God's standard, what hope do we have of seeing His eternal kingdom?

Apply

As a born-again Christian, how would you describe your relationship with God?

How would you explain what it means to be "justified by faith" to someone who is not familiar with the Bible?

How does knowing that you are justified by God's free gift of grace bless and encourage you?

Romans 3:21–31 Scriptures for Memorization/Meditation

For all have sinned and come short of the glory of God.
VERSE 23

Therefore we conclude that a man is justified
by faith without the deeds of the law.
VERSE 28

Verses for Further Memorization/Meditation

- For by grace you are saved through faith, and that not of yourselves; it is the gift of God, not of works, lest any man should boast (Ephesians 2:8–9).
- That being justified by His grace, we should be made heirs according to the hope of eternal life (Titus 3:7).
- There is neither Jew nor Greek, there is neither slave nor free, there is neither male nor female. For you are all one in Christ Jesus (Galatians 3:28).

Study 7

ROMANS 4:1–13

As the original patriarch of the Hebrew nation, Abraham holds a special place in the hearts of the Jewish people, and Christians as well. He is still revered as an example of righteous living. Not only that, but he is also an Old Testament example of what many mistakenly believe is a New Testament concept: justification by faith.

Justification is an unmerited, free gift of God that is the result of faith, not works (see Ephesians 2:8–9). This is reflected in Genesis 15:6, which says that Abraham, then known as Abram, "believed in the LORD, and He counted it to him for righteousness."

In Romans 4:1–13, Paul applies the truths and blessings of the life of Abraham to New Testament Christians, showing us that our justification is based on faith alone, not our own works.

ROMANS 4:1–13 STUDY OUTLINE

(VERSES 1–3)	Abraham was justified by faith, not by his works
(VERSES 4–5)	The difference between grace and works
(VERSES 6–8)	David and justification through faith
(VERSES 9–12)	Abraham was declared righteous *before* he was circumcised
(VERSE 13)	God's promise to Abraham was based on faith alone

By Faith, Not Works

1What then shall we say that Abraham our father has found as pertaining to the flesh? 2For if Abraham were justified by works, he would have had something to boast about, but not before God. 3For what does the scripture say? "Abraham believed God, and it was counted to him for righteousness."

4Now to him who works, the reward is counted not as grace but as debt. 5But to him who does not work, but believes in Him who justifies the ungodly, his faith is counted for righteousness, 6even as David also describes the blessedness of the man to whom God imputes righteousness without works, 7saying: "Blessed are those whose iniquities are forgiven and whose sins are covered. 8Blessed is the man to whom the Lord will not impute sin."

9Does this blessedness then come only on the circumcised or also on the uncircumcised? For we say that faith was counted to Abraham as righteousness. 10How then was it counted? When he was circumcised or uncircumcised? Not in circumcision, but in uncircumcision. 11And he received the sign of circumcision, a seal of the righteousness of the faith that he had yet being uncircumcised, that he might be the father of all those who believe, though they are not circumcised, that righteousness might be imputed to them also, 12and the father of circumcision to those who are not of the circumcision only, but who also walk in the steps of the faith of our father Abraham, which he had being yet uncircumcised. 13For the promise that he would be the heir of the world was not to Abraham or to his descendants through the law but through the righteousness of faith.

Observe

How do Jewish people view Abraham? Why do they hold him in such high regard?

Why could Abraham not glory in his justification before God?

Was Abraham counted as righteous *before* he was circumcised, or *after* he was circumcised? Why is that important?

Interpret

Why do you think Paul held up Abraham as an example of justification by faith?

What does the Bible mean when it says, "Abraham believed God, and it was counted to him for righteousness"?

Why does God respond to our faith and not our works of the law?

Apply

What might need to change so you can effectively follow the example Abraham set for a life of faith?

When you tell others about Jesus, how do you explain what God has done for you and why?

In what ways can you grow your faith and trust in the God who always keeps His promises?

Romans 4:1–13 Scriptures for Memorization/Meditation

For if Abraham were justified by works, he would have had something to boast about, but not before God. For what does the scripture say? "Abraham believed God, and it was counted to him for righteousness."
Verses 2–3

For the promise that he would be the heir of the world was not to Abraham or to his descendants through the law but through the righteousness of faith.
Verse 13

Verses for Further Memorization/Meditation

- And he believed in the Lord, and He counted it to him for righteousness (Genesis 15:6).
- For He has made Him who knew no sin to be sin for us, that we might be made the righteousness of God in Him (2 Corinthians 5:21).
- But without faith it is impossible to please Him, for he who comes to God must believe that He is, and that He is a rewarder of those who diligently seek Him (Hebrews 11:6).

Study 8

ROMANS 4:14–25

Abraham's justification before God was based on the principle of faith, not on the law or works. This passage gives a good (and simple) definition of the kind of faith God honors when it says that Abraham was "fully persuaded that [God] was able also to perform what He had promised" (Romans 4:21). It was because of that faith that Abraham received what God had promised.

Paul finishes this passage by telling us that God's promises are "also for us, to whom it shall be imputed if we believe in Him who raised up Jesus our Lord from the dead, who was delivered for our offenses and was raised again for our justification" (verses 24–25). The Christian life, starting with our salvation, is based on us believing that God keeps all His promises.

Romans 4:14–25 Study Outline

(verses 14–15)	The efficacy of faith
(verse 16)	Justification through God's grace, through faith
(verses 17–18)	The power of the God Abraham believed
(verses 19–22)	The look of Abraham's faith
(verses 23–25)	Abraham's justification is for us today

Justification by Faith

14 For if those who are of the law are heirs, faith is made void
and the promise is made of no effect, 15 because the law works
wrath. For where there is no law, there is no transgression.
16 Therefore it is by faith, that it might be by grace, to the end
that the promise might be secure to all the descendants, not
only to those who are of the law but also to those who are
of the faith of Abraham, who is the father of us all 17 (as it is
written, "I have made you a father of many nations") before
Him in whom he believed, even God, who revives the dead and
calls those things that are not as though they were.

18 Who against hope believed in hope, that he might become
the father of many nations, according to what was spoken:
"So shall your descendants be." 19 And not being weak in faith,
he did not consider his own body now dead, when he was
about a hundred years old, nor even the deadness of Sarah's
womb. 20 He did not stagger at the promise of God through
unbelief but was strong in faith, giving glory to God 21 and
being fully persuaded that He was able also to perform what
He had promised. 22 And therefore "it was imputed to him for
righteousness."

23 Now it was not written for his sake alone that it was
imputed to him, 24 but also for us, to whom it shall be imputed
if we believe in Him who raised up Jesus our Lord from the
dead, 25 who was delivered for our offenses and was raised
again for our justification.

Observe

According to Romans 4:15, what does the law bring to those who live by it?

What was God's promise to Abraham, according to Romans 4:18?

How was Abraham able to resist the temptation to doubt God's promise (see Romans 4:20)?

Interpret

Why, according to Romans 4:14–15, would God's promise be of no worth if a person had to keep the law perfectly to receive it?

According to Romans 4:19, what facts might have caused Abraham to doubt God's promise of a son?

What did Abraham believe about God that led him to complete faith?

Apply

How do you believe Abraham's righteousness by faith applies to you? How does Paul relate Abraham's example to you as a Christian?

What would eventually happen if you tried to be justified by keeping the law? What is the result of believing God's promise of justification by faith instead?

What do you normally do when faced with a choice between trusting God or focusing on your life situations? How can your faith help you stay hopeful and expectant?

Romans 4:14–25 Scripture for Memorization/Meditation

Now it was not written for his sake alone that it was imputed to him, but also for us, to whom it shall be imputed if we believe in Him who raised up Jesus our Lord from the dead, who was delivered for our offenses and was raised again for our justification.
VERSES 23–25

Verses for Further Memorization/Meditation

- "And as Moses lifted up the serpent in the wilderness, even so the Son of Man must be lifted up, that whoever believes in Him should not perish but have eternal life" (John 3:14–15).
- And He said to her, "Your sins are forgiven." And those who sat for dinner with Him began to say to themselves, "Who is this who also forgives sins?" And He said to the woman, "Your faith has saved you. Go in peace" (Luke 7:48–50).
- But you continue in the things that you have learned and have been assured of, knowing from whom you have learned them, and that from childhood you have known the holy scriptures, which are able to make you wise for salvation through faith that is in Christ Jesus (2 Timothy 3:14–15).

Study 9

ROMANS 5:1–11

The greatest benefit of justification by faith is undoubtedly that we have peace with God. We, people who were estranged from God and headed to a terrible place where we would be separated from Him for all eternity, are now at peace with Him—reconciled to Him—and destined for a forever home in heaven with Him.

But God's promises aren't just for where we end up for all eternity; they apply to us in this present time, even as we endure the difficulties of life in the present (verses 3–4).

God's love for us reaches back through eternity past. That's why Paul wrote that "while we were still sinners, Christ died for us" (verse 8).

What an act of love that truly is!

Romans 5:1–11 Study Outline

(VERSES 1–2)	The benefits of believing
(VERSES 3–4)	Promises for the present time
(VERSE 5)	The presence of the Holy Spirit
(VERSES 6–8)	God's love for us
(VERSES 9–11)	Salvation from God's wrath

Results of Justification

[1]Therefore, being justified by faith, we have peace with God through our Lord Jesus Christ, [2]by whom we also have access by faith into this grace in which we stand and rejoice in hope of the glory of God.

[3]And not only so, but we also glory in tribulations, knowing that tribulation works patience, [4]and patience experience, and experience hope. [5]And hope does not make us ashamed, because the love of God has been poured out in our hearts by the Holy Spirit who was given to us.

[6]For when we were still without strength, in due time Christ died for the ungodly. [7]For one will scarcely die for a righteous man, yet perhaps for a good man some would even dare to die. [8]But God demonstrates His love toward us, in that while we were still sinners, Christ died for us.

[9]Much more then, being now justified by His blood, we shall be saved from wrath through Him. [10]For if when we were enemies we were reconciled to God by the death of His Son, much more, being reconciled, we shall be saved by His life. [11]And not only so, but we also rejoice in God through our Lord Jesus Christ, by whom we have now received the atonement.

Observe

What is the result of being justified by faith, according to Romans 5:1–2?

What does Paul say about our approach to trials and tribulations in this passage?

What was humankind's condition when Jesus died on the cross for us?

Interpret

Why, according to Romans 5:5, will hope not make us ashamed?

What does Paul mean that we exult in hope of the glory of God?

From what are we saved when we are justified by faith?

Apply

What does it mean to you to have peace with God?

How and why can you now "rejoice in hope of the glory of God?"

How do you normally respond when faced with a problem or difficulty? Do you try to learn and grow from it, or do you try to escape it by any means necessary?

Romans 5:1–11 Scriptures for Memorization/Meditation

Therefore, being justified by faith, we have peace with God through our Lord Jesus Christ, by whom we also have access by faith into this grace in which we stand and rejoice in hope of the glory of God.
VERSES 1–2

But God demonstrates His love toward us, in that while we were still sinners, Christ died for us.
VERSE 8

Verses for Further Memorization/Meditation

- You will keep him whose mind is steadfast on You in perfect peace because he trusts in You (Isaiah 26:3).
- "He who believes in Him is not condemned, but he who does not believe is condemned already because he has not believed in the name of the only begotten Son of God" (John 3:18).
- "I am the resurrection and the life. He who believes in Me, though he were dead, yet shall he live. And whoever lives and believes in Me shall never die" (John 11:25–26).

Study 10

ROMANS 5:12–21

Romans 5:12–21 describes the spread of sin throughout humanity due to the actions of one man, Adam (see Genesis 3), and contrasts it with the work of a second man, the Lord Jesus Christ. He came to earth to die on the cross to remedy the problem of the sin that separated all humankind from their Creator.

It was Adam's disobedience that brought sin into the world and threw all creation into chaos. From that time forward, every human ever born was infected with sin and rebellion. But on the same day that Adam and his wife, Eve, sinned, God promised to send a Messiah, a man who would defeat sin once and for all.

Sin brought death, but Jesus brought new life.

Romans 5:12–21 Study Outline

(VERSE 12)	Through one man, sin infected the human race
(VERSES 13–14)	Sin brought death to humanity
(VERSES 15–19)	Contrasts between Adam and Jesus
(VERSES 20–21)	The law and God's grace

Death in Adam, Life in Christ

12 Therefore, as through one man sin entered into the world,
and death through sin, and so death passed on to all men, for
all have sinned— 13 for until the law sin was in the world, but
sin is not imputed when there is no law. 14 Nevertheless death
reigned from Adam to Moses, even over those who had not
sinned according to the likeness of Adam's transgression, who
is the figure of Him who was to come.

15 But the free gift is not like the offense. For if many died
through the offense of one, much more have the grace of
God and the gift by grace that is by one man, Jesus Christ,
abounded to many. 16 And the gift is not like what came
through one who sinned. For the judgment was through
one to condemnation, but the free gift is of many offenses
to justification. 17 For if by one man's offense death reigned
through one, much more shall those who receive abundance
of grace and of the gift of righteousness reign in life through
one, Jesus Christ.

18 Therefore, as judgment came on all men to condemna-
tion through the offense of one, even so the free gift came
on all men to justification of life through the righteousness
of one. 19 For as through one man's disobedience many were
made sinners, so through the obedience of one many shall
be made righteous.

20 Moreover the law entered, that the offense might abound.
But where sin abounded, grace abounded much more, 21 that,
as sin has reigned to death, even so grace might reign through
righteousness to eternal life through Jesus Christ our Lord.

Observe

Who is Paul referring to when he repeatedly uses the phrase "one man" in this passage?

What did Adam's disobedience bring to humankind?

Where sin abounded, according to Romans 5:20, what abounded much more?

Interpret

Who was the "one" referenced in Romans 5:19? What did this person do for humanity?

How would you rewrite verse 21 in your own words?

How does the power of the law to bring death through sin contrast with the power of God's grace to bring life?

Apply

What part does the Law of Moses play in your life as a believer?

How has God's grace blessed you? In what ways do you see it every day?

What would you say reigns in your life: sin leading to death, or grace leading to righteousness?

Romans 5:12–21 Scriptures for Memorization/Meditation

For if many died through the offense of
one, much more have the grace of God
and the gift by grace that is by one man,
Jesus Christ, abounded to many.
VERSE 15

For as through one man's disobedience many
were made sinners, so through the obedience
of one many shall be made righteous.
VERSE 19

Verses for Further Memorization/Meditation

- And so it is written, "The first man Adam was made a living soul." The last Adam was made a reviving spirit. However, what is spiritual is not first, but what is natural, and afterward what is spiritual. The first man was from the earth, earthly; the second man is the Lord from heaven (1 Corinthians 15:45–47).
- [God] has delivered us from the power of darkness and has translated us into the kingdom of His dear Son, in whom we have redemption through His blood, even the forgiveness of sins (Colossians 1:13–14).
- Who is a God like You, who pardons iniquity and passes by the transgression of the remnant of His heritage? He does not retain His anger forever, because He delights in mercy (Micah 7:18).

Study 11

ROMANS 6:1–10

God demonstrated His love when He sent Jesus to earth to die a sacrificial death and atone for the sin of everyone who comes to Him in faith, believing and receiving new life.

One of the results of that new life is a certain kind of death—death to sin. Paul wrote in this passage that we as believers would not continue in sin. "How shall we who are dead to sin live any longer in it?" Paul asks rhetorically. He taught the Roman Christians that they were now dead to sin and should live in newness of life, knowing they would live with Jesus for all eternity.

Romans 6:1–10 Study Outline

(VERSE 1)	Sin and God's grace
(VERSE 2)	Dying to sin
(VERSES 3–4)	Baptism: an illustration of the believer's death to sin
(VERSES 5–10)	The meaning of our death and resurrection with Jesus

Dead to Sin

1What shall we say then? Shall we continue in sin that grace
may abound? 2God forbid! How shall we who are dead to sin
live any longer in it? 3Do you not know that so many of us who
were baptized into Jesus Christ were baptized into His death?
4Therefore we were buried with Him by baptism into death,
that just as Christ was raised up from the dead by the glory
of the Father, even so we also should walk in newness of life.

5For if we have been planted together in the likeness of
His death, we shall also be in the likeness of His resurrection,
6knowing this, that our old man was crucified with Him, that
the body of sin might be destroyed, that hereafter we should
not serve sin. 7For he who has died has been freed from sin.

8Now if we have died with Christ, we believe that we shall
also live with Him, 9knowing that Christ, being raised from
the dead, dies no more. Death no longer has dominion over
Him. 10For in that He died, He died to sin once, but in that He
lives, He lives to God.

Observe

What do the first two verses of this passage say about believers continuing in sin?

How are we as believers to "walk" after we've come to faith in Christ?

What happened when Christ was bodily raised from the dead?

Interpret

What does it mean to be baptized into Christ's death?

What did Paul mean when he wrote that "our old man was crucified with Him?" What died at that crucifixion?

Why does dying with Christ lead to true life?

Apply

What part do you believe literal baptism played in your salvation?

How does this passage help shape your thinking concerning sin?

What steps can you take to identify and defeat sin in your life?

ROMANS 6:1–10 SCRIPTURES FOR MEMORIZATION/MEDITATION

What shall we say then? Shall we continue in sin that grace may abound? God forbid! How shall we who are dead to sin live any longer in it?
VERSES 1–2

Now if we have died with Christ, we believe that we shall also live with Him, knowing that Christ, being raised from the dead, dies no more.
VERSES 8–9

VERSES FOR FURTHER MEMORIZATION/MEDITATION

- If we confess our sins, He is faithful and just to forgive us our sins and to cleanse us from all unrighteousness (1 John 1:9).
- Whoever is born of God does not commit sin, for His seed remains in him, and he cannot sin, because he is born of God (1 John 3:9).
- Submit yourselves, therefore, to God. Resist the devil and he will flee from you. Draw near to God and He will draw near to you. Cleanse your hands, you sinners, and purify your hearts, you double-minded (James 4:7–8).

Study 12

ROMANS 6:11–23

In Romans 6:11–23, Paul promises that when we die to sin, we are made "alive to God through Jesus Christ our Lord." This presents each of us with an important choice: will we be servants of sin or servants of righteousness? This means we must choose one master: either Christ or our sinful selves. If Jesus is our Master, we will live in righteousness, but if we choose to be our own master, our lives will be governed by sin.

The Lord is not just our perfect Master but also our loving heavenly Father, our protector, and our source of comfort, strength, and blessing. Not only that, we can live lives as heirs of His eternal kingdom too.

That is the new life, the abundant life Jesus promised those who faithfully follow Him.

Romans 6:11–23 Study Outline

(VERSES 11–12)	Our death and our resurrection with Jesus
(VERSES 13–14)	Not under the law but under grace
(VERSE 15)	Shall we continue in sin because we are not under the law?
(VERSES 16–18)	No longer slaves to sin but servants of righteousness
(VERSES 19–23)	Remaining free in Christ

By Yielding the New Life to God

[11]Likewise you also consider yourselves to be dead indeed to
sin but alive to God through Jesus Christ our Lord. [12]Therefore
do not let sin reign in your mortal body, that you should obey
it in its lusts. [13]Do not yield the parts of your body to sin as
instruments of unrighteousness, but yield yourselves to God
as those who are alive from the dead, and the parts of your
body as instruments of righteousness to God. [14]For sin shall
not have dominion over you, for you are not under the law
but under grace.

[15]What then? Shall we sin because we are not under the
law but under grace? God forbid! [16]Do you not know that the
one to whom you yield yourselves as servants to obey, you
are his servants to whom you obey, whether of sin to death,
or of obedience to righteousness? [17]But thanks be to God, that
you were the servants of sin, but you have obeyed from the
heart that form of doctrine that was delivered to you. [18]Having
been made free from sin, then, you became the servants of
righteousness.

[19]I speak according to the manner of men because of the
infirmity of your flesh. For as you have yielded the parts of
your body as servants to uncleanness and to iniquity and more
iniquity, even so now yield the parts of your body as servants
to righteousness for holiness.

[20]For when you were the servants of sin, you were free from
righteousness. [21]What fruit did you have then in those things
of which you are now ashamed? For the end of those things is
death. [22]But now, having been made free from sin and having
become servants of God, you have your fruit to holiness and
the end, everlasting life. [23]For the wages of sin is death, but
the gift of God is eternal life through Jesus Christ our Lord.

Observe

What does Paul tell us we are dead to—and alive to?

To what does this passage encourage you to yield yourself?

What are the wages of sin? What is the gift of God?

Interpret

What does it mean to be a servant of sin? What about a servant of righteousness?

Why, according to Romans 6:14, does sin no longer have authority over the believer?

Why is it important that we obey "from the heart"? Is God more concerned with our actions or with our attitudes?

Apply

Why is it so important to not continue a life of sin after you've come to Jesus in faith? What are some ways you fight temptation?

What does it mean to you to be a servant of righteousness?

How can you walk that out daily?

Romans 6:11–23 Scriptures for Memorization/Meditation

Likewise you also consider yourselves to be dead indeed to sin but alive to God through Jesus Christ our Lord. Therefore do not let sin reign in your mortal body, that you should obey it in its lusts.
VERSES 11–12

But thanks be to God, that you were the servants of sin, but you have obeyed from the heart that form of doctrine that was delivered to you. Having been made free from sin, then, you became the servants of righteousness.
VERSES 17–18

For the wages of sin is death, but the gift of God is eternal life through Jesus Christ our Lord.
VERSE 23

Verses for Further Memorization/Meditation

- Put to death therefore the parts of your body that are on the earth: fornication, uncleanness, inordinate affection, evil desire, and covetousness, which is idolatry, for these things' sake the wrath of God comes on the children of disobedience, in which you also formerly walked when you lived in them (Colossians 3:5–7).
- Now thanks be to God, who always causes us to triumph in Christ, and through us makes evident the fragrance of His knowledge in every place (2 Corinthians 2:14).
- "For the eyes of the Lord are on the righteous, and His ears are open to their prayers, but the face of the Lord is against those who do evil" (1 Peter 3:12).

Study 13

ROMANS 7:1–12

As Christians, we are freed from the law, free from its condemnation and penalties. Were we under its jurisdiction, then we would be obligated to follow it perfectly to satisfy its demands in order to please God.

However, through faith in Christ, we are no longer under the bonds of the law but now living under grace, under the love of our heavenly Father. Now, we can live lives that please Him out of love and not out of legal obligation.

That is what freedom in Christ truly means.

Romans 7:1–12 Study Outline

(VERSES 1–3)	The law's authority over the living
(VERSE 4)	Dead to the law
(VERSE 5)	The limitations of the law
(VERSE 6)	Delivered from the law
(VERSES 7–9)	The purpose of the law
(VERSES 10–12)	Sin corrupts the law and brings death

Delivered from the Law

1Do you not know, brothers (for I speak to those who know the law), how the law has dominion over a man as long as he lives? 2For the woman who has a husband is bound by the law to her husband as long as he lives. But if the husband is dead, she is released from the law of her husband. 3So then she shall be called an adulteress if she is married to another man while her husband lives. But if her husband is dead, she is free from that law, so that she is not an adulteress, though she is married to another man.

4Therefore, my brothers, you also have become dead to the law through the body of Christ, that you should be married to another, even to Him who was raised from the dead, that we should bring forth fruit to God. 5For when we were in the flesh, the passions of sins, which were by the law, worked in the parts of our body to bring forth fruit to death. 6But now we have been delivered from the law, that being dead in what we had been held, that we should serve in newness of the Spirit and not in the oldness of the letter.

7What shall we say then? Is the law sin? God forbid! No, I would not have known sin but by the law. For I would not have known lust unless the law had said, "You shall not covet." 8But sin, taking opportunity by the commandment, worked in me all manner of strong desire. For without the law sin was dead.

9For I was once alive without the law, but when the commandment came, sin revived and I died. 10And the commandment, which was ordained to life, I found to be to death. 11For sin, taking opportunity by the commandment, deceived me and by it slew me. 12Therefore the law is holy, and the commandment holy and just and good.

Observe

What is the relationship between the Christian and the law?

What does this passage teach about marriage? How does this affect your view of it?

In Romans 7:6, what is the new way in which we serve God?

Interpret

What does Paul mean when he writes, "the law has dominion over a man as long as he lives"?

Why are we made to "die to the law"? Does that mean we no longer need to obey God's principles?

What can we learn about sin in Romans 7:8–11?

Apply

Why is it important to understand God's law from the Old Testament?

When temptation arrives, how do you usually respond? What helps you stand strong against it?

Since you are not under the authority of the law, under what authority do you live?

Romans 7:1–12 Scripture for Memorization/Meditation

But now we have been delivered from the law, that being dead in what we had been held, that we should serve in newness of the Spirit and not in the oldness of the letter.
Verse 6

Verses for Further Memorization/Meditation

- "Do not think that I have come to destroy the Law or the Prophets. I have come not to destroy but to fulfill" (Matthew 5:17).
- The law of the Lord is perfect, converting the soul. The testimony of the Lord is sure, making wise the simple. The statutes of the Lord are right, rejoicing the heart. The commandment of the Lord is pure, enlightening the eyes. The fear of the Lord is clean, enduring forever. The judgments of the Lord are true and righteous altogether (Psalm 19:7–9).
- And we have all received of His fullness, and grace for grace. For the law was given by Moses, but grace and truth came by Jesus Christ (John 1:16–17).

Study 14

ROMANS 7:13–25

Paul opens this passage by explaining the role of the law in the life of the believer. He then addresses the struggle a person faces when attempting to live a godly life apart from the empowerment of God.

Paul discusses the challenge we humans face in our struggle against sin. When we come to Christ in faith, God forgives our sins and takes up residence within us in the person of the Holy Spirit. And though we are no longer slaves to sin, the sinful nature remains, leading us to the spiritual tension that we all feel.

So what is Paul's solution? Jesus Christ is the only way for us to enjoy victory over sin, setting us free from the body of death.

Romans 7:13–25 Study Outline

(VERSE 13)	The law exposes sin
(VERSE 14)	The spiritual law cannot restrain a sinful human
(VERSES 15–19)	Struggling to obey in our own strength
(VERSES 20–23)	An inner battle
(VERSE 24)	Paul's desperate struggle
(VERSE 25)	Looking to Jesus

Strife between Two Natures

[13]Was then what is good made death to me? God forbid! But
sin, that it might appear sin, working death in me by what is
good, that by the commandment sin might become exceed-
ingly sinful. [14]For we know that the law is spiritual, but I am
carnal, sold under sin.

[15]For what I do, I do not understand. For I do not do what
I want to do, but I do what I hate. [16]If, then, I do what I do not
want to do, I consent to the law that it is good. [17]Now then it is
no longer I who do it, but sin that dwells in me.

[18]For I know that no good thing dwells in me (that is, in my
flesh). For the will is present with me, but I do not find how to
perform what is good. [19]For I do not do the good that I want,
but I do the evil that I do not want. [20]Now if I do what I do
not want, it is no longer I who do it, but sin that dwells in me.

[21]I find then a law that when I want to do good, evil is
present with me. [22]For I delight in the law of God according
to the inner man, [23]but I see another law in the parts of my
body, warring against the law of my mind and bringing me into
captivity to the law of sin that is in the parts of my body. [24]O
wretched man that I am! Who shall deliver me from the body
of this death? [25]I thank God through Jesus Christ our Lord.
So then, with the mind I myself serve the law of God, but with
the flesh, the law of sin.

Observe

What does Paul say about the nature of the law and what it reveals about sin (see Romans 7:13–14)?

How does Paul describe his inner conflict in Romans 7:14?

To what universal struggle does Paul give voice in Romans 7:15?

Interpret

What does Romans 7:14 say about why we humans are unable to fulfill the law's requirements?

What did Paul mean when he wrote, "I do not do what I want to do, but I do what I hate" (see Romans 7:15, 19)?

What was the solution to Paul's (and our) conflict (see Romans 7:25)?

Apply

In this spiritual struggle, would you say your life more often reflects a desire to please God or yourself?

Why is it so important to understand that only in Christ, not our own efforts, can we find rescue from the power of sin?

When you've fallen into temptation, what do you usually do next?

Romans 7:13–25 Scripture for Memorization/Meditation

For I delight in the law of God according to the inner man, but I see another law in the parts of my body, warring against the law of my mind and bringing me into captivity to the law of sin that is in the parts of my body.
Verses 22–23

Verses for Further Memorization/Meditation

- The sting of death is sin, and the strength of sin is the law. But thanks be to God, who gives us the victory through our Lord Jesus Christ (1 Corinthians 15:56–57).
- No temptation has taken you but such as is common to man. But God is faithful, who will not allow you to be tempted above what you are able, but with the temptation will also make a way of escape, that you may be able to bear it (1 Corinthians 10:13).
- And besides this, giving all diligence, add to your faith, virtue; and to virtue, knowledge; and to knowledge, self-control; and to self-control, patience; and to patience, godliness; and to godliness, brotherly kindness; and to brotherly kindness, love (2 Peter 1:5–7).
- I am crucified with Christ; nevertheless, I live, yet not I, but Christ lives in me, and the life that I now live in the flesh I live by the faith of the Son of God, who loved me and gave Himself for me (Galatians 2:20).

Study 15

ROMANS 8:1–13

Romans 8 opens with the assurance that those whose faith is in Jesus Christ no longer need to fear God's punishment for their sins. Why? Because Jesus took that punishment on Himself when He died a horrible, painful death on a wooden cross.

This passage moves on to address the futility of trying to live the Christian life in the flesh instead of in and through the Spirit of God. Verses 9–11 then explain how we are empowered when we live in the Holy Spirit, concluding: "He who raised up Christ from the dead shall also revive your mortal bodies by His Spirit who dwells in you."

Romans 8:1–13 Study Outline

(VERSE 1)	No condemnation
(VERSES 2–4)	Life in the Spirit versus life in the flesh
(VERSES 5–8)	The futility of trying to please God in the flesh
(VERSES 9–11)	Empowered to live in the Spirit
(VERSES 12–13)	Indebted to the Spirit, not the flesh

Life in the Spirit

1Therefore there is now no condemnation for those who are in
Christ Jesus, who walk not according to the flesh but according
to the Spirit. 2For the law of the Spirit of life in Christ Jesus
has made me free from the law of sin and death. 3For what the
law could not do, in that it was weak through the flesh, God
did by sending His own Son in the likeness of sinful flesh and
for sin: He condemned sin in the flesh, 4that the righteousness
of the law might be fulfilled in us who walk not according to
the flesh but according to the Spirit.

5For those who are according to the flesh think about
the things of the flesh, but those who are according to the
Spirit, the things of the Spirit. 6For to be carnally minded is
death, but to be spiritually minded is life and peace, 7because
the carnal mind is enmity against God, for it is not subject to
the law of God nor indeed can be. 8So then, those who are in the
flesh cannot please God.

9But you are not in the flesh but in the Spirit, if indeed
the Spirit of God dwells in you. Now if any man does not have
the Spirit of Christ, he is not His. 10And if Christ is in you, the
body is dead because of sin, but the Spirit is life because of
righteousness. 11But if the Spirit of Him who raised up Jesus
from the dead dwells in you, He who raised up Christ from
the dead shall also revive your mortal bodies by His Spirit
who dwells in you.

12Therefore, brothers, we are debtors, not to the flesh, to
live according to the flesh. 13For if you live according to the
flesh, you shall die, but if through the Spirit you put to death
the deeds of the body, you shall live.

Observe

For whom is there now no condemnation?

How is the mind that's set on the flesh different from the mind set on the Spirit (see Romans 8:6–8)?

According to Romans 8:13, what makes the difference between spiritual life and spiritual death?

Interpret

What does it mean to be "in Christ Jesus"?

What is the difference between the law of sin and death and the law of the Spirit of life?

How, according to Romans 8:5, are those who walk according to the Spirit different from those who walk according to the flesh?

Apply

When have you felt like a "debtor" to the flesh? Why?

What does it mean to walk in the flesh versus walking in the Spirit?

How can you "put to death the deeds of the body" through the Spirit?

Romans 8:1–13 Scriptures for Memorization/Meditation

Therefore there is now no condemnation for those
who are in Christ Jesus, who walk not according
to the flesh but according to the Spirit.
VERSE 1

But if the Spirit of Him who raised up Jesus from
the dead dwells in you, He who raised up Christ
from the dead shall also revive your mortal
bodies by His Spirit who dwells in you.
VERSE 11

Verses for Further Memorization/Meditation

- "I, even I, am He who blots out your transgressions for My own sake and will not remember your sins" (Isaiah 43:25).
- "For God did not send His Son into the world to condemn the world but that the world might be saved through Him" (John 3:17).
- "Search the scriptures, for in them you think you have eternal life. And these are they that testify of Me" (John 5:39).
- "Truly, truly, I say to you, he who hears My word and believes in Him who sent Me has everlasting life, and shall not come into condemnation but has passed from death to life" (John 5:24).

Study 16

ROMANS 8:14–21

In Romans 8:14–15, Paul describes life as a child of God. It's an intimate, joyful relationship with God the Father, one in which the Christian has the privilege of relating to the almighty, holy Creator in the most familiar of terms: *Abba*.

Paul then goes on to state that "The Spirit Himself bears witness with our spirit that we are the children of God" and then addresses the role suffering plays in the life of a true child of God. Life in the Spirit, he writes, helps us to understand and endure suffering.

Romans 8:14–21 Study Outline

(VERSES 14–15)	Living as children of God
(VERSE 16)	The evidence we are children of God
(VERSES 17–18)	Suffering for Christ's sake
(VERSES 19–21)	Creation anticipating coming glory

The Results of the Gospel

[14]For as many as are led by the Spirit of God, they are the sons
of God. [15]For you have not received the spirit of bondage again
to fear, but you have received the Spirit of adoption, by whom
we cry, "Abba, Father!" [16]The Spirit Himself bears witness with
our spirit that we are the children of God, [17]and if children,
then heirs—heirs of God and joint heirs with Christ, if indeed
we suffer with Him, that we may also be glorified together.

[18]For I consider that the sufferings of this present time
are not worthy to be compared with the glory that shall
be revealed in us. [19]For the earnest expectation of the cre-
ation waits for the revealing of the sons of God. [20]For the cre-
ation was made subject to vanity, not willingly, but because
of Him who has subjected the same in hope, [21]because the
creation itself also shall be delivered from the bondage of
corruption into the glorious liberty of the children of God.

Observe

Who are the rightful children of God, according to Romans 8:14?

What allows us to address God as “Abba, Father”?

In Romans 8:18, what does Paul contrast with our present sufferings?

Interpret

What does "Abba Father" literally mean?

How does the Spirit Himself bear witness that we are the children of God (Romans 8:16)?

What are those led by God's Spirit called in Romans 8:14? What all does that imply?

Apply

What types of "spirit" exist? Which have you received?

What about this passage gives you a sense of hope?

How does knowing that you have a place in your loving heavenly Father's eternal kingdom comfort and sustain you in times of suffering here on earth?

Romans 8:14–21 Scriptures for Memorization/Meditation

For as many as are led by the Spirit of God, they are the sons of God. For you have not received the spirit of bondage again to fear, but you have received the Spirit of adoption, by whom we cry, "Abba, Father!"
VERSES 14–15

For I consider that the sufferings of this present time are not worthy to be compared with the glory that shall be revealed in us.
VERSE 18

Verses for Further Memorization/Meditation

- He has made us accepted in the Beloved, in whom we have redemption through His blood, the forgiveness of sins, according to the riches of His grace (Ephesians 1:6–7).
- I acknowledged my sin to You, and my iniquity I have not hidden. I said, "I will confess my transgressions to the Lord," and You forgave the iniquity of my sin (Psalm 32:5).
- Bless the Lord, O my soul, and do not forget all His benefits, who forgives all your iniquities, who heals all your diseases, who redeems your life from destruction, who crowns you with loving-kindness and tender mercies (Psalm 103:2–4).

Study 17

ROMANS 8:22–34

Paul wrote in this passage that all creation—including each of us—anticipates the coming glory when our adoption into God's eternal kingdom is complete and our bodies are redeemed.

These things are the earnest expectations of those whose faith is in the Lord Jesus Christ. In the meantime, God promises to help us in many ways, including our lives of prayer. In Romans 8:28, a well-known and much-beloved verse, Paul also promises that our loving heavenly Father makes all things work together for our good and His glory.

Finally, Paul writes wonderful words of comfort and assurance concerning God's faithfulness to His children in Christ.

Romans 8:22–34 Study Outline

(VERSES 22–25)	Waiting with perseverance
(VERSES 26–27)	God's present help through the Spirit
(VERSES 28–30)	God works all things for good
(VERSE 31)	A comforting promise: God is for us
(VERSE 32)	The gift of Jesus Christ
(VERSES 33–34)	Jesus' present ministry

Hope and Assurance in Christ

22For we know that the whole creation groans and labors in pain together until now. 23And not only that, but also we ourselves who have the firstfruits of the Spirit, even we ourselves groan within ourselves, waiting for the adoption—namely, the redemption of our body. 24For we are saved by hope, but hope that is seen is not hope. For why does a man still hope for what he sees? 25But if we hope for what we do not see, then we wait for it with patience.

26Likewise the Spirit also helps our infirmities. For we do not know what we should pray for as we ought, but the Spirit Himself makes intercession for us with groanings that cannot be uttered. 27And He who searches the hearts knows what the mind of the Spirit is, because He makes intercession for the saints according to the will of God.

28And we know that all things work together for good to those who love God, to those who are the called according to His purpose. 29For those whom He foreknew, He also predestined to be conformed to the image of His Son, that He might be the firstborn among many brothers. 30Moreover those whom He predestined, He also called, and those whom He called, He also justified, and those whom He justified, He also glorified.

31What then shall we say to these things? If God is for us, who can be against us? 32He who did not spare His own Son but delivered Him up for us all, how shall He not also with Him freely give us all things? 33Who shall bring anything to the charge of God's elect? It is God who justifies. 34Who is he who condemns? It is Christ who died, yes, rather, who was raised again, who is even at the right hand of God, who also makes intercession for us.

Observe

What does Paul say we groan for within ourselves?

Who intercedes for us when we don't know how to pray as we should?

According to Romans 8:29–30, what has God predestined for those who are His in Christ?

Interpret

What do we believers have as we await the redemption of our bodies (Romans 8:23)? What does that mean?

In Romans 8:24–25, what does the word *hope* mean?

What does this passage mean by the word *intercession*?

Apply

How can you wait patiently for the ultimate redemption you do not yet have?

How can you grow your faith so that you can live in God's promise and trust that He works "all things" together for your good?

What role does the Holy Spirit play in your life as a believer?

Romans 8:22–34 Scriptures for Memorization/Meditation

Likewise the Spirit also helps our infirmities. For we do not know what we should pray for as we ought, but the Spirit Himself makes intercession for us with groanings that cannot be uttered.
Verse 26

And we know that all things work together for good to those who love God, to those who are the called according to His purpose.
Verse 28

Who is he who condemns? It is Christ who died, yes, rather, who was raised again, who is even at the right hand of God, who also makes intercession for us.
Verse 34

Verses for Further Memorization/Meditation

- Behold, what manner of love the Father has bestowed on us, that we should be called the sons of God (1 John 3:1).
- Therefore He is also able to save to the uttermost those who come to God through Him, since He always lives to make intercession for them (Hebrews 7:25).
- Let your conduct be without covetousness, and be content with the things that you have, for He has said, "I will never leave you or abandon you." So we may boldly say, "The Lord is my helper, and I will not fear what man shall do to me" (Hebrews 13:5–6).

Study 18

ROMANS 8:35–39

Earlier, Paul promised the Roman Christians that they were indeed beloved children of the living God, freed from the possibility of future condemnation. Now, in this passage, Paul assures them—and us—that nothing would ever change that. Nothing—including spiritual opposition, persecution, or other difficulties—could separate us from God's love in Jesus Christ. He wrote these things at a time when followers of Christ faced intense persecution for their faith. God loves us, he wrote, and because He loves us, we are "more than conquerors" in the face of intense, overwhelming opposition.

Romans 8:35–39 Study Outline

(VERSE 35)	Christ's steadfast love for us
(VERSES 36–37)	More than conquerors
(VERSES 38–39)	What can separate us from Christ's love? Nothing!

Security in Christ

35 Who shall separate us from the love of Christ? Shall tribula-
tion, or distress, or persecution, or famine, or nakedness, or
peril, or sword? 36 As it is written: "For Your sake we are killed
all day long; we are accounted as sheep for the slaughter."
37 No, in all these things we are more than conquerors through
Him who loved us.

38 For I am persuaded that neither death nor life, nor angels
nor principalities nor powers, nor things present nor things
to come, 39 nor height nor depth, nor any other creature shall
be able to separate us from the love of God that is in Christ
Jesus our Lord.

Observe

What things cannot separate believers from the love of Christ, according to Romans 8:35?

How does Paul describe believers who endure serious difficulties in Romans 8:37?

What was Paul convinced that neither death nor life could separate believers from (Romans 8:38–39)?

Interpret

Why would Paul list all these difficulties for the Roman Christians in this passage?

What kinds of difficulties were the Roman believers apparently facing when Paul wrote the words?

Does this passage imply that the Roman believers (or us) would ever cease having problems in this life?

Apply

How does being called "more than a conqueror" affect your walk of faith?

What kinds of difficulties have you faced in this life? How does this passage encourage you to remain steadfast as you endure hard times?

How do you respond when you've prayed for deliverance, but your difficulties continue? What advice would you give others in the same place?

Romans 8:35–39 Scriptures for Memorization/Meditation

No, in all these things we are more than
conquerors through Him who loved us.
Verse 37

For I am persuaded that neither death nor life,
nor angels nor principalities nor powers, nor things
present nor things to come, nor height nor depth,
nor any other creature shall be able to separate us
from the love of God that is in Christ Jesus our Lord.
Verses 38–39

Verses for Further Memorization/Meditation

- He who dwells in the secret place of the Most High shall abide under the shadow of the Almighty. I will say of the Lord, "He is my refuge and my fortress. My God, in Him I will trust" (Psalm 91:1–2).
- "My sheep hear My voice, and I know them, and they follow Me. And I give eternal life to them, and they shall never perish, nor shall any man pluck them out of My hand" (John 10:27–28).
- I have written these things to you who believe in the name of the Son of God, that you may know that you have eternal life, and that you may believe in the name of the Son of God (1 John 5:13).

Study 19

ROMANS 9:1–24

Romans 9 is a shift in focus for Paul—from his assurances and promise to the Gentile Christians living in Rome to his sorrow and his heart's desire for his fellow Jews who did not accept the gospel message.

Though a great majority of his Jewish brethren did not accept the Messiah, Paul still held that God had not failed His children of promise—that they were the people God used to bring the Messiah into the world.

Paul sought to help the Roman Christians understand that God used all things—including the Israelites' unbelief—to bring His plans to fruition and to bring glory to Himself.

Romans 9:1–24 Study Outline

(VERSES 1–2)	Paul's sorrow
(VERSES 3–5)	The source of Paul's sorrow
(VERSES 6–9)	God has not failed His children of promise
(VERSES 10–13)	The example of Jacob and Esau
(VERSES 14–16)	God's righteous choices
(VERSES 17–18)	The example of Pharaoh
(VERSES 19–21)	Human responsibility
(VERSES 22–24)	God glorifies Himself as He sees fit

Paul's Heart for His Fellow Jews

1I say the truth in Christ. I do not lie, my conscience also bearing
me witness in the Holy Spirit, 2that I have great heaviness and
continual sorrow in my heart. 3For I could wish that I myself
were accursed from Christ for my brothers, my countrymen
according to the flesh, 4who are Israelites, to whom pertain the
adoption, and the glory, and the covenants, and the giving of
the law, and the service of God, and the promises, 5whose are
the fathers, and from whom, as concerning the flesh, Christ
came, who is over all, God blessed forever. Amen.

6It is not as though the word of God has taken no effect.
For they are not all Israel who are of Israel, 7nor are they all
children because they are the descendants of Abraham, but
"In Isaac your descendants shall be called." 8That is, those
who are the children of the flesh, they are not the children
of God, but the children of the promise are counted as the
descendants. 9For this is the word of promise: "At this time I
will come and Sarah shall have a son."

10And not only this, but when Rebekah also had conceived
by one man, even by our father Isaac 11(for the children being
not yet born, not having done any good or evil, that the pur-
pose of God according to election might stand, not by works
but by Him who calls), 12it was said to her, "The elder shall
serve the younger." 13As it is written, "Jacob I have loved, but
Esau I have hated."

14What shall we say then? Is there unrighteousness with
God? God forbid! 15For He says to Moses, "I will have mercy on
whom I will have mercy, and I will have compassion on whom
I will have compassion." 16So then it is not by him who wills
or by him who runs but by God, who shows mercy.

17For the scripture says to Pharaoh, "Even for this same
purpose I have raised you up, that I might show My power in
you, and that My name might be declared throughout all the
earth." 18Therefore He has mercy on whom He will have mercy,
and He hardens whom He wills.

[19]You will say to me then, "Why does He still find fault?
For who has resisted His will?" [20]No, but who are you, O man,
who replies against God? Shall the thing formed say to him
who formed it, "Why have you made me like this?" [21]Does the
potter not have power over the clay, to make from the same
lump one vessel to honor and another to dishonor?
[22]What if God, wanting to show His wrath and to make His
power known, endured with much long-suffering the vessels
of wrath fitted to destruction, [23]and that He might make known
the riches of His glory on the vessels of mercy, which He had
prepared beforehand for glory, [24]even us whom He has called,
not from the Jews only but also from the Gentiles?

Observe

What was the reason for Paul's great sorrow in Romans 9?

Who chose Jacob to receive God's special promises? On what basis was that choice made? Did it have anything to do with Jacob's character qualities?

Who does Paul say is the ultimate source of mercy and compassion?

Interpret

What did Paul mean when he wrote, "I could wish that I myself were accursed from Christ for my brothers, my countrymen according to the flesh?"

Why would God raise up an evil Pharaoh during the time of the Exodus?

What did God mean when He said, "Jacob I have loved, but Esau I have hated?"

Apply

Do you feel a sorrow like Paul felt for his Jewish brethren over the lost state of your friends, family members, ethnic group, or countrymen? What should such sorrow motivate you to do?

....

....

....

....

....

How would you describe God's mercy and compassion in your life to a nonbeliever?

....

....

....

....

....

How does this passage help you gain a deeper understanding of God and His unfailing love for humankind?

....

....

....

....

....

....

Romans 9:1–24 Scripture for Memorization/Meditation

That is, those who are the children of the flesh, they are not the children of God, but the children of the promise are counted as the descendants.
VERSE 8

Verses for Further Memorization/Meditation

- And Moses returned to the LORD and said, "Oh, these people have sinned a great sin and have made themselves gods of gold. Yet now, if You will forgive their sin—and if not, I ask You, blot me out of Your book that You have written" (Exodus 32:31–32).
- For the Lord will not reject forever. But though He causes grief, yet He will have compassion according to the multitude of His mercies (Lamentations 3:31–32).
- "For God so loved the world that He gave His only begotten Son, that whoever believes in Him should not perish but have everlasting life. For God did not send His Son into the world to condemn the world but that the world might be saved through Him" (John 3:16–17).
- "Say to them, 'As I live,' says the Lord GOD, 'I have no pleasure in the death of the wicked but that the wicked turn from his way and live. Turn, turn from your evil ways, for why will you die, O house of Israel?'" (Ezekiel 33:11).

Study 20

ROMANS 9:25–33

Paul begins this passage by quoting the Old Testament prophet Hosea in verse 25: "Those who were not My people I will call 'My people,' and her who was not beloved, 'beloved.'" This prophecy has been fulfilled in the person of Jesus Christ, who came to earth as the Messiah for Jews and Gentiles alike.

In verse 27, Paul also quotes these words from the book of Isaiah: "Though the number of the children of Israel is as the sand of the sea, a remnant shall be saved," which means that God would choose a certain number from among the nation of Israel to be saved through Jesus Christ.

Paul states that Israel had missed its long-awaited Messiah because the people had sought God's righteousness by works of the law instead of by faith.

Romans 9:25–33 Study Outline

(VERSES 25–26)	God's right to call those who were previously not His people
(VERSES 27–29)	A remnant among Israel will be saved
(VERSES 30–33)	Israel missed the Messiah because they failed to come by faith

The Prophets Foretold the Blinding of Israel

[25]As He says also in Hosea: "Those who were not My people I
will call 'My people,' and her who was not beloved, 'beloved.'"
[26]"And it shall come to pass that in the place where it was said
to them, 'You are not My people,' there they shall be called the
children of the living God." [27]Isaiah also cries concerning Israel:
"Though the number of the children of Israel is as the sand of
the sea, a remnant shall be saved. [28]For He will finish the work
and cut it short in righteousness, because the Lord will make a
short work on the earth." [29]And as Isaiah said before, "Unless
the Lord of Sabaoth had left us descendants, we would have
been like Sodom and been made like Gomorrah."

[30]What shall we say then? That the Gentiles, who did not
follow after righteousness, have attained righteousness, even
the righteousness that is by faith. [31]But Israel, who followed
after the law of righteousness, has not attained the law of
righteousness. [32]Why? Because they sought it not by faith
but, as it were, by the works of the law. For they stumbled at
that stumbling stone, [33]as it is written: "Behold, I lay in Zion a
stumbling stone and a rock of offense, and whoever believes
in Him shall not be ashamed."

Observe

What did Hosea say of the Gentiles, as Paul quoted in Romans 9:25?

In Romans 9:31, who does Paul say had not attained the law of righteousness?

What is the result for all who believe and trust in God (Romans 9:33)?

Interpret

How and why do Hosea's words—"Those who were not My people I will call 'My people,' and her who was not beloved, 'beloved'"—apply to Gentiles?

In Romans 9:30, what did the Gentiles do to attain righteousness?

Who is "that stumbling stone" in Romans 9:32? What does this name mean?

Apply

On what basis do you believe God saved you and called you righteous? Did it have anything to do with what you have done or will do?

What do you believe is the right approach to the law for a Christian?

What does this passage teach you about God's grace?

Romans 9:25–33 Scripture for Memorization/Meditation

As He says also in Hosea: "Those who were
not My people I will call 'My people,'
and her who was not beloved, 'beloved.'"
VERSE 25

Verses for Further Memorization/Meditation

- The LORD has appeared of old to me, saying, "Yes, I have loved you with an everlasting love; therefore with loving-kindness I have drawn you (Jeremiah 31:3).
- For we are His workmanship, created in Christ Jesus for good works, which God has before ordained that we should walk in them (Ephesians 2:10).
- But now this is what the LORD says, who created you, O Jacob, and He who formed you, O Israel: "Do not fear, for I have redeemed you. I have called you by your name. You are Mine" (Isaiah 43:1).
- The LORD your God in your midst is mighty. He will save; He will rejoice over you with joy. He will rest in His love; He will rejoice over you with singing (Zephaniah 3:17).

Study 21

ROMANS 10:1–13

The above passage speaks of how the people of Israel—the Jews—had rejected their Messiah and the message of salvation through Jesus Christ. Paul stated that he hoped and prayed that his people would turn to Jesus and away from their insistence on keeping the law for their salvation, for Jesus was the end of the law for those who come to Him in faith.

Paul wanted the Romans to understand the law had been ended in the sense that their perfect obedience to it was no longer the basis for their relationship with God, for their righteousness before Him.

This passage includes with Paul's declarations that "if you confess with your mouth the Lord Jesus and believe in your heart that God has raised Him from the dead, you shall be saved" (verse 9) and "whoever calls on the name of the Lord shall be saved" (verse 13).

Romans 10:1–13 Study Outline

(VERSES 1–3)	Israel failed to submit to God's righteousness
(VERSE 4–8)	God's righteousness versus human attempts at righteousness
(VERSES 9–13)	God's righteousness is gained by faith

God's Promises to Israel

[1]Brothers, my heart's desire and prayer to God for Israel is that
they might be saved. [2]For I bear them witness that they have
a zeal for God, but not according to knowledge. [3]For, being
ignorant of God's righteousness and going about to establish
their own righteousness, they have not submitted themselves
to the righteousness of God. [4]For Christ is the end of the law
for righteousness to everyone who believes.

[5]For Moses describes the righteousness that is of the law,
that the man who does those things shall live by them. [6]But
the righteousness that is of faith speaks in this way: "Do not
say in your heart, 'Who shall ascend into heaven?' (that is, to
bring Christ down from above) [7]or, 'Who shall descend into
the deep?' (that is, to bring up Christ again from the dead)."
[8]But what does it say? "The word is near you, even in your
mouth and in your heart" (that is, the word of faith that we
preach): [9]that if you confess with your mouth the Lord Jesus
and believe in your heart that God has raised Him from the
dead, you shall be saved. [10]For with the heart man believes
to righteousness, and with the mouth confession is made to
salvation. [11]For the scripture says: "Whoever believes in Him
shall not be ashamed." [12]For there is no difference between
the Jew and the Greek, for the same Lord over all is rich to
all who call on Him. [13]For "whoever calls on the name of the
Lord shall be saved."

Observe

What was Paul's desire and prayer for the Israelites?

According to Romans 10:4, who may receive righteousness?

What does this passage identify as a benefit to anyone who trusts in Jesus (Romans 10:11)?

Interpret

What does this passage teach about both Jews and Gentiles?

What does "righteousness that is of the law" (Romans 10:5) mean?

What two actions lead to salvation (Romans 10:9)? How do they relate to the Word of God?

Apply

How confident are you in your own salvation? Why?

When have you tried to rely on your own goodness (law-keeping) to be saved? How did that work out?

How have you experienced that God is "rich to all who call on Him" (Romans 10:12)?

Romans 10:1–13 Scriptures for Memorization/Meditation

For with the heart man believes to righteousness, and with the mouth confession is made to salvation. For the scripture says: "Whoever believes in Him shall not be ashamed."
VERSES 10–11

For there is no difference between the Jew and the Greek, for the same Lord over all is rich to all who call on Him. For "whoever calls on the name of the Lord shall be saved."
VERSES 12–13

Verses for Further Memorization/Meditation

- But we are all like an unclean thing, and all our righteousness is as filthy rags. And we all fade like a leaf, and our iniquities, like the wind, have taken us away (Isaiah 64:6).
- "Because you say, 'I am rich and increased with goods and have need of nothing'—and do not know that you are wretched and miserable and poor and blind and naked—I counsel you to buy from Me gold refined in the fire, that you may be rich, and white clothing, that you may be clothed, and that the shame of your nakedness does not appear, and anoint your eyes with eye salve, that you may see" (Revelation 3:17–19).
- Not by works of righteousness that we have done, but according to His mercy He saved us, by the washing of regeneration and renewing of the Holy Spirit, whom He poured out on us abundantly through Jesus Christ our Savior (Titus 3:5–6).

Study 22

ROMANS 11:1–10

Though Israel had rejected its Messiah, Paul states that didn't mean God had turned away from His chosen people. There is still an opportunity for Jewish people to be restored to fellowship with the Lord, and His plan was that a substantial remnant would be saved through faith in Jesus Christ.

Yes, Israel has rejected her Messiah, but God has not rejected Israel. There is still hope, the very same blessed hope offered to the rest of the world.

Romans 11:1–10 Study Outline

(VERSES 1–5)	The remnant of grace
(VERSES 6–10)	God chooses a remnant according to His grace

Spiritual Israel Is Finding Salvation

[1]I say then, has God rejected His people? God forbid! For I
also am an Israelite, of the descendants of Abraham, of the
tribe of Benjamin. [2]God has not rejected His people whom He
foreknew. Do you not know what the scripture says of Elijah,
how he makes intercession to God against Israel, saying, [3]"Lord,
they have killed Your prophets and destroyed Your altars, and
I alone am left, and they are seeking my life"?

[4]But what does the answer of God say to him? "I have
reserved for Myself seven thousand men who have not bowed
the knee to the image of Baal."

[5]Even so then, at this present time, there also is a remnant
according to the election of grace. [6]And if by grace, then it is
no longer of works; otherwise grace is no longer grace. But
if it is of works, then it is no longer grace; otherwise work is
no longer work.

[7]What then? Israel has not obtained what it seeks, but the
elect have obtained it and the rest were blinded. [8]According
to what is written, "God has given them the spirit of slumber,
eyes that they should not see and ears that they should not
hear, to this day." [9]And David says, "Let their table be made
a snare and a trap, and a stumbling block and a recompense
to them. [10]Let their eyes be darkened, that they may not see,
and bow down their back always."

Observe

What does Paul say God has not done concerning Israel?

Of what does Paul present himself as an example in Romans 11:1?

What was David's prayer, according to Romans 11:9–10?

Interpret

What does the word *remnant* mean in this passage? Who or what is this remnant?

What was Elijah's complaint in Romans 11:3, and what did it say about the heart condition of the people of Israel?

What does Paul mean by "the election of grace"?

Apply

Have you ever felt, like Elijah, that you were the only one of your family and friends who truly follows the Lord?

Do you believe that people can see the benefits of believing the gospel of Jesus Christ by how you live your life?

Why is it important to pray for and witness to the unsaved?

Romans 11:1–10 Scripture for Memorization/Meditation

And if by grace, then it is no longer of works; otherwise grace is no longer grace. But if it is of works, then it is no longer grace; otherwise work is no longer work.
VERSE 6

Verses for Further Memorization/Meditation

- But God has revealed them to us by His Spirit. For the Spirit searches all things, yes, the deep things of God. For what man knows the things of a man, except the spirit of man that is in him? Even so no man knows the things of God but the Spirit of God (1 Corinthians 2:10–11).
- Be a partaker of the afflictions of the gospel according to the power of God, who has saved us and called us with a holy calling, not according to our works, but according to His own purpose and grace, which was given to us in Christ Jesus before the world began (2 Timothy 1:8–9).
- For the LORD has poured out on you the spirit of deep sleep and has closed your eyes. The prophets and your rulers, the seers He has covered (Isaiah 29:10).

Study 23

ROMANS 12:1–8

Paul encouraged the Christians in Rome to offer up not just their bodies, but their lives and will to God as a "living sacrifice." They were to give up their entire being for God to do with as He desired.

He wants that same sacrifice from believers today.

The apostle also encouraged those in the Roman church to resist conforming to the world and instead allow God to transform their minds so their thinking would reflect the "good and acceptable and perfect will of God."

Finally, in this passage, Paul encouraged humility for the Romans, for God loves a humble heart and resists the proud. That meekness would serve the believers well as they each played a part in ministering to one another.

Romans 12:1–8 Study Outline

(VERSE 1)	The living sacrifice
(VERSE 2)	Transformation through Jesus Christ
(VERSE 3)	Live in humility
(VERSES 4–5)	Unity and diversity in the body of Christ
(VERSES 6–8)	Using the gifts God has given individual believers

Christian Life and Service

1 Therefore I beseech you, brothers, by the mercies of God, that you present your bodies as a living sacrifice, holy, acceptable to God, which is your reasonable service. 2 And do not be conformed to this world, but be transformed by the renewing of your mind, that you may prove what is that good and acceptable and perfect will of God.

3 For through the grace given to me I say to every man who is among you not to think of himself more highly than he ought to think, but to think soberly, according to the measure of faith God has dealt to every man. 4 For as we have many parts in one body and all parts do not have the same function, 5 so we, being many, are one body in Christ, and each one is a member of the others.

6 Having then differing gifts according to the grace that is given to us: whether prophecy, let us prophesy according to the proportion of faith; 7 or ministry, let us attend to our ministering; or he who teaches, on teaching; 8 or he who exhorts, on exhortation; he who gives, let him do it with simplicity; he who rules, with diligence; he who shows mercy, with cheerfulness.

Observe

What does Paul tell the Romans to make of themselves (Romans 12:1)?

How should believers approach the world they live in (Romans 12:2)?

What spiritual gifts are listed in Romans 12:6–8?

Interpret

What exactly is a sacrifice? How can Christians be "living" sacrifices?

What does Paul mean when he writes, "be transformed by the renewing of your mind?" How does this transformation take place?

What words come to mind when you read Paul's warning against thinking of ourselves "more highly than [we] ought to think?"

Apply

ROMANS 12:1–8

What does it mean to you to offer your body as a "living sacrifice?" What would be the result of doing that?

In what ways do you find yourself being "conformed to this world?" What needs to change?

How have you seen God renew your mind? What part can you play in the process?

Romans 12:1–8 Scriptures for Memorization/Meditation

Therefore I beseech you, brothers, by the mercies of God, that you present your bodies as a living sacrifice, holy, acceptable to God, which is your reasonable service.
VERSE 1

And do not be conformed to this world, but be transformed by the renewing of your mind, that you may prove what is that good and acceptable and perfect will of God.
VERSE 2

Verses for Further Memorization/Meditation

- What, do you not know that your body is the temple of the Holy Spirit, who is in you, whom you have from God, and you are not your own? For you were bought with a price. Therefore glorify God in your body and in your spirit, which are God's (1 Corinthians 6:19–20).
- Now may the God of peace, who brought back from the dead our Lord Jesus, that great shepherd of the sheep, through the blood of the everlasting covenant, make you perfect in every good work to do His will, working in you what is well pleasing in His sight, through Jesus Christ, to whom be glory forever and ever. Amen (Hebrews 13:20–21).
- Do not love not world or the things that are in the world. If any man loves the world, the love of the Father is not in him. For all that is in the world—the lust of the flesh, and the lust of the eyes, and the pride of life—is not of the Father but is of the world (1 John 2:15–16).

Study 24

ROMANS 12:9–21

Jesus taught at length about loving others—even those we might well consider our "enemies." In Romans 12:9–21, Paul echoes Jesus' teaching on this subject, starting with, "Let love be without hypocrisy." The Roman Christians were to love one another—and those outside the faith—in a genuine way.

We too are to care about other believers in an authentic way. We should, as the apostle John wrote, "love one another, for love is of God, and everyone who loves is born of God and knows God" (1 John 4:7). Not only that, but we are to love those who aren't in the Lord's family. We shouldn't hold hateful or vengeful attitudes toward anyone, even those who have wronged or persecuted us.

Romans 12:9–21 Study Outline

(VERSES 9–13)	The look of Christian family love
(VERSE 14)	Loving those outside the faith
(VERSES 15–21)	Dealing with all people

The Look of Real Love

9Let love be without hypocrisy. Hate what is evil; cling to what
is good. 10Be kindly affectionate to one another with brotherly
love, preferring one another in honor, 11not slothful in business,
fervent in spirit, serving the Lord, 12rejoicing in hope, patient
in tribulation, continuing persistently in prayer, 13distributing
to the needs of the saints, given to hospitality.

14Bless those who persecute you. Bless, and do not curse.
15Rejoice with those who rejoice, and weep with those who
weep. 16Be of the same mind toward one another. Do not think
about high things, but associate with men of low position. Do
not be wise in your own opinions.

17Do not repay evil for evil to any man. Provide honest
things in the sight of all men. 18If it is possible, as much as it
lies in you, live peaceably with all men.

19Do not avenge yourselves, dearly beloved, but rather
give place to wrath, for it is written, "Vengeance is Mine. I will
repay," says the Lord. 20Therefore, "If your enemy is hungry,
feed him; if he is thirsty, give him a drink. For in so doing you
shall heap coals of fire on his head." 21Do not be overcome by
evil, but overcome evil with good.

Observe

What must love be without, according to Romans 12:9?

What are believers to hate, and what are they to cling to, according to this passage?

How are Christians to respond to persecution and other mistreatment?

Interpret

What does it mean to be "kindly affectionate to one another with brotherly love, preferring one another in honor"?

Why does Paul instruct the Romans to "associate with men of low position"? What attitude does this reflect?

How can Christians "overcome evil with good"?

Apply

In what practical ways can you bless those who persecute you for your faith?

What does it mean to you to "Hate what is evil; cling to what is good"? How can you live this out every day?

What can and should you do when you feel want to take vengeance on someone who has wronged you?

Romans 12:9–21 Scriptures for Memorization/Meditation

Let love be without hypocrisy.
Hate what is evil; cling to what is good.
VERSE 9

Bless those who persecute you.
Bless, and do not curse. Rejoice with those who rejoice, and weep with those who weep.
VERSES 14–15

Verses for Further Memorization/Meditation

- Do not rejoice when your enemy falls, and do not let your heart be glad when he stumbles, lest the Lord see it, and it displease Him, and He turn away His wrath from him (Proverbs 24:17–18).
- Finally, be all of one mind, having compassion for one another, love as brothers, be sympathetic, be courteous, not rendering evil for evil or reviling for reviling, but on the contrary, blessing, knowing that you are called to this, that you should inherit a blessing (1 Peter 3:8–9).
- "But love your enemies, and do good, and lend, hoping for nothing back. And your reward shall be great, and you shall be the children of the Highest. For He is kind to the unthankful and to the evil" (Luke 6:35).

Study 25

ROMANS 13:1–7

Paul, as well as other New Testament writers and Jesus Himself, had some things to say about how Christians should relate to civil authority. Should believers submit and obey without reservation? Or are there times for disobedience—as Peter and John indicated in the book of Acts?

In Romans 13:1–7, Paul instructs the Roman believers to be subject to governing authorities, for they are ultimately appointed by God and play a purpose in His plan. Sometimes, this is to bless the people, but sometimes, it's to bring judgment.

Romans 13:1–7 Study Outline

(VERSES 1–2)	The proper response to legitimate government authority
(VERSES 3–4)	The role of government
(VERSES 5–7)	Our responsibility toward government

Submit to Governing Authorities

1 Let every soul be subject to the higher authorities. For there
is no authority but by God, and the authorities that exist are
ordained by God. 2 Therefore whoever resists authority resists
the ordinance of God, and those who resist shall receive con-
demnation for themselves. 3 For rulers are not a terror to good
works, but to the evil. Will you then not be afraid of the one
in authority? Do what is good and you shall have praise from
the same, 4 for he is the minister of God to you for good. But if
you do what is evil, be afraid, for he does not bear the sword
in vain. For he is the minister of God, an avenger to execute
wrath on him who does evil.

5 Therefore you need to be subject, not only for wrath
but also for the sake of conscience. 6 For this reason you also
pay taxes, for they are God's ministers attending continually
on this very thing. 7 Therefore render to all their due: tax to
whom tax is due, custom to whom custom, fear to whom fear,
honor to whom honor.

Observe

Why does Paul say in Romans 13:1 to "be subject to the higher authorities"?

According to Romans 13:2, what does rebellion against human authority amount to? What is its result?

What does Paul instruct the Roman believers to do in Romans 13:6–7?

Interpret

How are civil authorities a "minister of God to you for good" (Romans 13:4)?

What does Romans 13:5 mean when it tells believers to be subject to authority "not only for wrath but also for the sake of conscience"?

In the book of Acts, the apostles resisted authority by continuing to preach the gospel. Why would God not consider that a problem?

Apply

In what ways—even relatively insignificant ways—have you found yourself in resistance to governing authorities?

If governing authorities instituted laws that violated your conscience when it came to honoring biblical commandments and principles, how would you respond?

In what ways can you show respect for authority while still voicing opposition when you know they are in the wrong?

Romans 13:1–7 Scripture for Memorization/Meditation

Let every soul be subject to the higher authorities. For there is no authority but by God, and the authorities that exist are ordained by God. Therefore whoever resists authority resists the ordinance of God, and those who resist shall receive condemnation for themselves.

VERSES 1–2

Verses for Further Memorization/Meditation

- Submit yourselves to every ordinance of man for the Lord's sake, whether it be to the king as supreme or to governors as to those who are sent by him for the punishment of evildoers and for the praise of those who do good (1 Peter 2:13–14).
- I exhort therefore, first of all, that supplications, prayers, intercessions, and giving of thanks be made for all men, for kings and for all who are in authority, that we may lead a quiet and peaceful life in all godliness and honesty. For this is good and acceptable in the sight of God our Savior (1 Timothy 2:1–3).
- Put them in mind to be subject to principalities and powers, to obey magistrates, to be ready for every good work, to speak evil of no man, to be not brawlers but gentle, showing all meekness to all men (Titus 3:1–2).

Study 26

ROMANS 13:8–14

One day, Jesus was asked a particularly loaded question: "Master, which is the great commandment in the law?" (Matthew 22:36). Jesus answered, "'You shall love the Lord your God with all your heart, and with all your soul, and with all your mind.' This is the first and great commandment. And the second is like it: 'You shall love your neighbor as yourself.' On these two commandments hang all the Law and the Prophets" (22:37–40).

In Romans 13:8, Paul wrote something that reflected well Jesus' words above: "Owe no man anything but to love one another, for he who loves another has fulfilled the law."

Love is our obligation to our neighbors. It is the one thing each of us is commanded to do, both in word and in deed. It is, according to Paul, the only "debt" we are to carry and the one debt we can repay daily.

Romans 13:8–14 Study Outline

(VERSES 8–10) Love: the Christian obligation

(VERSES 11–14) Loving others and walking with God

Love Fulfills the Law

8 Owe no man anything but to love one another, for he who loves
another has fulfilled the law. 9 For this, “You shall not commit
adultery,” “You shall not kill,” “You shall not steal,” “You shall
not bear false witness,” “You shall not covet,” and if there is
any other commandment, it is briefly comprehended in this
saying—namely, “You shall love your neighbor as yourself.”
10 Love works no ill to his neighbor; therefore love is the ful-
filling of the law.

11 And knowing the time, that now it is high time to awake
out of sleep. For now our salvation is nearer than when
we believed. 12 The night is far spent; the day is at hand.
Therefore let us cast off the works of darkness, and let us
put on the armor of light. 13 Let us walk honestly, as in the
day, not in rioting and drunkenness, not in sexual immorality
and wantonness, not in strife and envying. 14 But put on the
Lord Jesus Christ, and do not make provision for the flesh,
to fulfill its lusts.

Observe

Why is love the singular thing we owe to other people (Romans 13:8)?

According to Romans 13:8–10, how does love behave, and what does it accomplish?

With what important instruction does Paul conclude this passage?

Interpret

What does it mean to "fulfill the law"? Why is that important?

What does "love your neighbor as yourself" mean?

Why does Paul tell the Roman Christians (and all of us) to "awake out of sleep" (Romans 13:11)?

Apply

In what specific ways can you be purposeful to love others around you?

How can you not "make provision for the flesh, to fulfill its lusts"?

What does it mean to you to "put on the Lord Jesus Christ?" How can you do that daily?

Romans 13:8–14 Scriptures for Memorization/Meditation

Owe no man anything but to love one another,
for he who loves another has fulfilled the law.
VERSE 8

But put on the Lord Jesus Christ, and do not make
provision for the flesh, to fulfill its lusts.
VERSE 14

Verses for Further Memorization/Meditation

- Jesus said to him, "'You shall love the Lord your God with all your heart, and with all your soul, and with all your mind.' This is the first and great commandment. And the second is like it: 'You shall love your neighbor as yourself.' On these two commandments hang all the Law and the Prophets" (Matthew 22:37–40).
- Put on, therefore, as the elect of God, holy and beloved, hearts of mercies, kindness, humbleness of mind, meekness, long-suffering, being patient with one another and forgiving one another if any man has a quarrel against any. Even as Christ forgave you, so you also do" (Colossians 3:12–13).
- Also flee youthful lusts, but follow righteousness, faith, love, peace with those who call on the Lord out of a pure heart (2 Timothy 2:22).

Study 27

ROMANS 14:1–13

In Romans 14, Paul addresses an apparent tension between Roman Christians. They had conflicting opinions and convictions over certain activities that are not clearly defined as sinful in scripture—so how believers should view them in light of their freedom in Christ? Was it permissible for these Christians to eat meat? What about observing Jewish holy days and Sabbaths?

Paul described those who thought of certain foods or other items as inherently sinful as being "weak in the faith." But instead of condemning these believers, Paul addressed those who were stronger in the faith, commanding them to welcome their weaker brothers and sisters into the church community.

Romans 14:1–13 Study Outline

(VERSES 1–2)	Receiving the weaker believer
(VERSES 3–6)	Don't judge members of the family
(VERSES 7–9)	We live and die to the Lord
(VERSES 10–13)	All will face judgment before Jesus

Addressing Doubtful/ Questionable Things

[1]Receive him who is weak in the faith, but not to doubtful disputes. [2]For one believes that he may eat all things; another who is weak eats vegetables. [3]Do not let him who eats despise him who does not eat, and do not let him who does not eat judge him who eats, for God has received him. [4]Who are you who judges another man's servant? To his own master he stands or falls. Yes, he shall be upheld, for God is able to make him stand.

[5]One man esteems one day above another; another esteems every day alike. Let every man be fully persuaded in his own mind. [6]He who regards the day, regards it to the Lord, and he who does not regard the day, to the Lord he does not regard it. He who eats, eats to the Lord, for he gives God thanks. And he who does not eat, to the Lord he does not eat and gives God thanks. [7]For none of us lives to himself, and no man dies to himself. [8]For whether we live, we live to the Lord, and whether we die, we die to the Lord. Therefore whether we live or die, we are the Lord's. [9]For to this end Christ died and rose and revived, that He might be Lord of both the dead and living.

[10]But why do you judge your brother? Or why do you despise your brother? For we shall all stand before the judgment seat of Christ. [11]For it is written: "'As I live,' says the Lord, 'every knee shall bow to Me and every tongue shall confess to God.'" [12]So then every one of us shall give account of himself to God. [13]Therefore let us not judge one another anymore, but rather judge this: that no man should put a stumbling block or an occasion to fall in his brother's way.

Observe

In Romans 14:1, whom does Paul say believers should accept? In the following verses, what does Paul say the Roman Christians should not pass judgment on?

What differences of opinion does Paul cite as questionable matters in this passage?

What is Paul's overarching point of this passage (Romans 14:7–9)?

Interpret

Why would the Roman Christians have divided over eating meats or vegetables?

What role should thankfulness to God play in our convictions and decision-making (Romans 14:6–7)?

Why should believers not judge one another (Romans 14:10–13)?

Apply

What attitude should you have toward those whose convictions may vary from your own?

What issues are nonnegotiable for Christian fellowship? Why?

Why, according to Romans 14:10, should you not look down on others?

Romans 14:1–13 Scriptures for Memorization/Meditation

For none of us lives to himself, and no man dies to himself. For whether we live, we live to the Lord, and whether we die, we die to the Lord. Therefore whether we live or die, we are the Lord's.
VERSES 7–8

For it is written: "'As I live,' says the Lord, 'every knee shall bow to Me and every tongue shall confess to God.'" So then every one of us shall give account of himself to God.
VERSES 11–12

Verses for Further Memorization/Meditation

- All things are lawful for me, but not all things are expedient. All things are lawful for me, but not all things edify. Let no man seek his own, but each man another's well-being (1 Corinthians 10:23–24).
- "Therefore, in all things, whatever you want men to do to you, do even so to them, for this is the Law and the Prophets" (Matthew 7:12).
- Let nothing be done through strife or boastfulness, but in lowliness of mind let each esteem others better than themselves. Look not every man on his own things, but every man also on the things of others (Philippians 2:3–4).
- For, brothers, you have been called to liberty; only do not use liberty for an occasion to the flesh, but by love serve one another (Galatians 5:13).

Study 28

ROMANS 14:14–23

At the start of this passage, Paul asserts that believers need to be mindful of the sensitive consciences of others when they engage in certain questionable activities. Even if one individual's conscience isn't troubled by something, it is not loving to continue in that activity if it offends another believer.

Instead, Paul wrote, believers should prioritize love and concern for one another's spiritual well-being. This means pursuing a higher calling, namely using their liberty in Christ to build up others, not tear them down—even unintentionally. The bottom line, he wrote, is that believers should do all things in faith.

Romans 14:14–23 Study Outline

(VERSES 14–15) Don't make your brothers and sisters stumble

(VERSES 16–18) The higher call of the kingdom of God

(VERSES 19–21) Use your liberty to build up one another

(VERSES 22–23) Doing all things in faith

Preserving the Work of God in Others

[14]I know and am persuaded by the Lord Jesus that there is
nothing unclean in itself, but to him who esteems anything
to be unclean, to him it is unclean. [15]But if your brother is
grieved with your food, now you are not walking in love. Do
not destroy with your food him for whom Christ died. [16]Then
do not let your good be spoken of as evil, [17]for the kingdom of
God is not food and drink but righteousness and peace and joy
in the Holy Spirit. [18]For he who serves Christ in these things
is acceptable to God and approved by men. [19]Therefore let
us follow after the things that make for peace, and things by
which one may edify another.

[20]Do not destroy the work of God for food. All things indeed
are pure, but it is evil for that man who eats with offense. [21]It is
good neither to eat meat nor to drink wine nor to do anything
by which your brother stumbles or is offended or is made weak.
[22]Do you have faith? Keep it to yourself before God. Happy is
he who does not condemn himself in that thing that he allows.
[23]And he who doubts is condemned if he eats, because he does
not eat by faith. For whatever is not of faith is sin.

Observe

What did Paul say he was fully persuaded of (Romans 14:14)?

What does Paul say we should never do by the food we eat (Romans 15:15)?

In Romans 14:17, what does Paul say the kingdom of God is about—and not about?

Interpret

What is the result of serving Christ in righteousness, peace, and joy (Romans 14:18)?

Why is it good "neither to eat meat nor to drink wine" if another Christian struggles with your freedom to do so?

What does Paul say we Christians should strive to do (Romans 14:19)? Why is that?

Apply

What activities or practices do you believe might cause another believer to stumble? What will you do—or not do—concerning those things?

How can you know whether something you may partake in offends your brother or sister in Christ?

How can you discern whether any questionable activity (for example, drinking in moderation) is permissible for you?

Romans 14:14–23 Scriptures for Memorization/Meditation

Then do not let your good be spoken of as evil, for the kingdom of God is not food and drink but righteousness and peace and joy in the Holy Spirit.
VERSES 16–17

Do you have faith? Keep it to yourself before God. Happy is he who does not condemn himself in that thing that he allows. And he who doubts is condemned if he eats, because he does not eat by faith. For whatever is not of faith is sin.
VERSES 22–23

Verses for Further Memorization/Meditation

- For there is one God and one mediator between God and men, the man Christ Jesus, who gave Himself as a ransom for all (1 Timothy 2:5–6).
- To us there is but one God, the Father, from whom are all things, and we in Him, and one Lord Jesus Christ, by whom are all things, and we through Him (1 Corinthians 8:6).
- Then he called for a light and sprang in, and came trembling and fell down before Paul and Silas, and brought them out and said, "Sirs, what must I do to be saved?" And they said, "Believe in the Lord Jesus Christ, and you shall be saved, and your house" (Acts 16:29–31).

Study 29

ROMANS 15:1–13

Paul begins Romans 15 by placing a more positive spin on the issue of doubtful or questionable things he had written earlier in his letter. He knows there is much more to Christian love and fellowship than avoiding offending or judging others. Here, he focuses on how the Roman Christians could help one another to grow in their faith. He instructs them to "bear the frailties of the weak" and to be patient with those who are not strong in their faith. Their goal, he wrote, was to follow Jesus' example as they pleased and edified one another. And Paul encouraged them toward like-mindedness with one another.

ROMANS 15:1–13 STUDY OUTLINE

(VERSES 1–2)	Care and concern for others
(VERSES 3–4)	Jesus' example
(VERSES 5–6)	Paul's prayer for the Romans
(VERSES 7–13)	Love, joy, and peace

The Law of Love Concerning Doubtful Things

1We, then, who are strong ought to bear the frailties of the
weak, and not to please ourselves. 2Let every one of us please
his neighbor for his good, for edification. 3For even Christ did
not please Himself, but as it is written: "The reproaches of those
who reproached You fell on Me." 4For whatever things were
written formerly were written for our learning, that through
patience and comfort from the scriptures we might have hope.
5Now may the God of patience and consolation grant you to
be like-minded toward one another, according to Christ Jesus,
6that with one mind and one mouth you may glorify God, even
the Father of our Lord Jesus Christ.

7Therefore receive one another, as Christ also received
us, to the glory of God. 8Now I say that Jesus Christ was a
minister of the circumcision for the truth of God, to confirm
the promises made to the fathers, 9and that the Gentiles might
glorify God for His mercy, as it is written: "For this reason I will
confess to You among the Gentiles and sing to Your name."
10And again he says: "Rejoice, you Gentiles, with His people!"
11And again: "Praise the Lord, all you Gentiles, and laud Him,
all you people!" 12And again, Isaiah says: "There shall be a root
of Jesse, and He who shall rise to reign over the Gentiles, in
Him the Gentiles shall trust."

13Now may the God of hope fill you with all joy and peace
in believing, that you may abound in hope through the power
of the Holy Spirit.

Observe

What does Paul say those strong in the faith should bear with?

How did Jesus set an example for us, according to Romans 15:3?

How should the Gentiles—the vast majority of our world—respond to God's mercy?

Interpret

What, according to Romans 15:2, should we seek to please our neighbors and not ourselves? Why?

Why was the scripture written down in the past (Romans 15:4)? What does it do for us?

Why does Paul want believers to accept one another (Romans 15:7)? What does that accomplish?

Apply

In what specific ways can you show kindness to fellow believers today?

What does it mean to you to "glorify God, even the Father of our Lord Jesus Christ"? How can you live that out every day?

What does Paul pray the God of hope will fill you with (Romans 15:13)? How would this affect your life?

Romans 15:1–13 Scriptures for Memorization/Meditation

Let every one of us please his neighbor for his good, for edification. For even Christ did not please Himself, but as it is written: "The reproaches of those who reproached You fell on Me."
VERSES 2–3

Now may the God of patience and consolation grant you to be like-minded toward one another, according to Christ Jesus, that with one mind and one mouth you may glorify God, even the Father of our Lord Jesus Christ.
VERSES 5–6

Verses for Further Memorization/Meditation

- Let this mind be in you, which was also in Christ Jesus, who, being in the form of God, thought it not robbery to be equal with God but made Himself of no reputation and took on Himself the form of a servant and was made in the likeness of men (Philippians 2:5–7).
- Bear one another's burdens, and so fulfill the law of Christ (Galatians 6:2).
- "But whoever wants to be great among you shall be your minister, and whoever of you wants to be the first shall be servant of all. For even the Son of Man came not to be ministered to, but to minister, and to give His life as a ransom for many" (Mark 10:43–45).

Study 30

ROMANS 15:14–33

Paul's closing remarks to the Roman church begin in Romans 15:14 and continue through to the end of chapter 16. In Romans 15:14–33, Paul seeks to unify the Roman Christians around his mission to advance the gospel of Jesus Christ, to let them know of his intent to visit them, and to request that they pray for him and his continued mission.

Paul opens this passage with glowing comments for the Romans and their relationships with one another as brothers and sisters in Christ. Paul knows that his work as the apostle to the Gentiles was not complete, and he continues by writing about his mission and how he wants it to progress.

Romans 15:14–33 Study Outline

(VERSES 14–16)	Paul's motivation
(VERSES 17–19)	The work God has done through Paul
(VERSES 20–21)	Paul's desire to preach the gospel in new places
(VERSES 22–24)	Paul's desire to visit the Christians in Rome
(VERSES 25–29)	Paul's present plans
(VERSES 30–33)	Paul's plea for prayer

Paul: the Minister to the Gentiles

14And I myself also am convinced of you, my brothers, that
you also are full of goodness, filled with all knowledge, also
able to admonish one another. 15Nevertheless, brothers, I have
written more boldly to you about some things, as reminding
you, because of the grace that was given to me by God, 16that
I should be the minister of Jesus Christ to the Gentiles, minis-
tering the gospel of God, that the offering up of the Gentiles
might be acceptable, being sanctified by the Holy Spirit.

17Therefore, I have something of which I may boast through
Jesus Christ in those things that pertain to God. 18For I will
not dare to speak of any of those things that Christ has not
worked through me to make the Gentiles obedient—by word
and deed, 19through mighty signs and wonders, by the power
of the Spirit of God—so that from Jerusalem and all around to
Illyricum I have fully preached the gospel of Christ.

20Yes, I have so labored to preach the gospel, not where
Christ was named, lest I should build on another man's foun-
dation, 21but as it is written: "Those to whom He was not
spoken of shall see, and those who have not heard shall
understand." 22For this reason I also have been much hindered
from coming to you.

23But now, no longer having a place in these parts, and
having a great desire these many years to come to you, 24I will
come to you whenever I take my journey to Spain. For I trust
to see you in my journey and to be brought on my way there
by you, if first I may be somewhat filled with your company.

25But now I am going to Jerusalem to minister to the saints.
26For it has pleased those of Macedonia and Achaia to make a
certain contribution for the poor saints who are in Jerusalem.
27It has truly pleased them, and they are their debtors. For
if the Gentiles have been made partakers of their spiritual
things, their duty is also to minister to them in material things.
28Therefore, when I have performed this and have sealed this
fruit to them, I will go by way of you to Spain. 29And I am sure

that when I come to you, I shall come in the fullness of the
blessing of the gospel of Christ.
30Now I beseech you, brothers, for the Lord Jesus Christ's
sake and for the love of the Spirit, that you strive together with
me in your prayers to God for me, 31that I may be delivered from
those in Judea who do not believe, and that my service that I
have for Jerusalem may be accepted by the saints, 32that I may
come to you with joy by the will of God and may be refreshed
with you. 33Now the God of peace be with you all. Amen.

Observe

Of what three things was Paul convinced concerning the Roman believers?

What did God's grace allow Paul to do?

Why was Paul planning to travel to Jerusalem?

Interpret

Why was Paul "the minister of Jesus Christ to the Gentiles" (Romans 15:16)?

Why would Paul prefer not to "build on another man's foundation" (Romans 15:20) in his ministry?

How did Paul urge the Romans to join him in his efforts?

Apply

How are the Gentiles sanctified, according to Romans 15:16? How does this happen in your life?

In what specific ways can you imitate Paul's witness and testimony to those around you?

How might you encourage other ministers in the ways the Romans did Paul?

Romans 15:14–33 Scripture for Memorization/Meditation

Yes, I have so labored to preach the gospel,
not where Christ was named, lest I should build
on another man's foundation, but as it is written:
"Those to whom He was not spoken of shall see,
and those who have not heard shall understand."
VERSES 20–21

Verses for Further Memorization/Meditation

- Preach the word. Be ready in season, out of season. Reprove, rebuke, exhort with all long-suffering and doctrine (2 Timothy 4:2).
- And He said to them, "Go into all the world and preach the gospel to every creature. He who believes and is baptized shall be saved, but he who does not believe shall be condemned" (Mark 16:15–16).
- Praying always with all prayer and supplication in the Spirit, and watching with all perseverance and supplication for all saints, and for me, that words may be given to me, that I may open my mouth boldly to make known the mystery of the gospel (Ephesians 6:18–19).
- "Therefore I say to you, whatever things you desire when you pray, believe that you receive them, and you shall have them" (Mark 11:24).